The Orvis
Wingshooting
Handbook

ORVIS

The Orvis
Wingshooting
Handbook
Fully Revised and Updated

Proven Techniques for Better Shotgunning

BRUCE BOWLEN

The Lyons Press
Guilford, Connecticut
An imprint of The Globe Pequot Press

The Lyons Press is an imprint of The Globe Pequot Press.

Illustrations by Rod Walinchus

Library of Congress Cataloging-in-Publication Data is available on file.

ISBN 978-1-59228-514-3

Printed in the United States of America

10 9 8 7 6 5 4

Contents

Introduction

Since 1973 I have been trying to help wingshooters improve their technique. My experience has convinced me of one thing: Most field gunners do not have a sense of what they are doing right or wrong, why they hit one bird but miss the next. The reason for their quandary lies in the fact that they have no clearly defined technique. All too often they adopt a fatalistic attitude toward their shooting. "He's a natural shot," or "I can't hit my hat today." They resign themselves to the whims of fate that seem to govern their shooting. One day they can't miss; the next day they can't hit the proverbial barn door.

But shooting is not governed by the fates. We can learn to improve our shooting skills and tailor our equipment to improve our odds. The all-too-prevalent attitude in this country is that good shots are born, not made. A very different attitude prevails in the United Kingdom. The British view wingshooting as a skill that can be learned. They consider wingshooting another of the eye-hand sports that has form or technique that can be developed with practice. Just as there is a right way and a wrong way to swing a golf club, there is a right way and a wrong way to swing a shotgun. Granting latitude for stylistic quirks, the British believe there is a method to field shooting. I have to side with the British. Good wing shots are not always born. You can learn to be a good shot. Not all of us are blessed with the same level of eye-hand coordination and timing, but we can all learn to improve our technique and hone our skills. What is important is that we understand the basics of good wingshooting and know how to practice productively.

The basic theory and style of shooting that will be outlined herein have been taken primarily from British sources. More specifically, I had the privilege of receiving personal instruction from Rex Gage, former director of the Holland and Holland Shooting School, and Michael Rose, senior instructor at the West London Shooting School. The foundation underlying the British approach, in my opinion, can be traced to Robert Churchill. Certainly *Churchill's Game Shooting*, by Macdonald Hasting, has been the greatest influence in my development as a shooter and an instructor. I make no pretext about having authored the theory or style. Over the course of thirty-plus years of instructing, I certainly developed my own means of conveying the message, but that message is Robert Churchill's.

I don't want to sound like an expatriate. I am not suggesting that U.S. shotgunners are inferior to their European counterparts. What is different in this country is the attitude toward shooting. Many American men feel as though it is part of our heritage to be good shots. They wouldn't think twice about asking a golf pro to help them with their swing, but many seem reticent to admit they could use some help when it comes to swinging a shotgun.

I do not consider myself to be a shooter of any special ability. My own natural gifts of coordination and timing are very ordinary. Somewhere along the way I have made all the mistakes a shotgunner could make. Only through diligence and practice have I been able to develop into a passable field shot. This statement is not made to be modest, but rather to give the reader an insight into my development as a wingshooter and an instructor. I believe that not being a gifted natural shot has made me a better instructor. The natural may have difficulty identifying and empathizing with a beginner's mistakes. Having made most of the mistakes myself, and having had the opportunity to look over the shoulders of shotgunners for more than thirty years, I have been given an insight into the problems encountered by field gunners. What has prompted me to write this book is the hope that it may help the average wingshooter overcome some of those problems. It is intended to be a concise guide for the field gunner, with the focus on shooting technique as opposed to hunting strategies. It certainly is not an exhaustive treatise on the subject. But I hope it will prove helpful to the field shooter in choosing equipment and developing a shooting style that will be practical and efficient.

By way of introduction, I tell the students who attend the Orvis Wingshooting Schools that we have three goals to accomplish during our sessions. First, I stress that safety is always the number one consideration and that we must always be mindful of the school's safety procedures. Second, we hope students will enjoy themselves and remember that wingshooting is to be enjoyed. Be able to accept a miss; don't allow a miss or two to make you fret and impede your enjoyment and your ability to learn. All too often students allow themselves to get so uptight over a miss or two that it becomes practically impossible for them to make progress in their technique. Third, we hope to make wingshooting as natural and as easy for every shooter as we possibly can. The style we teach is based on the Churchill method, but students bring their own sets of skills and experiences, and it is the job of the instructor to get the best outcome for each student.

A Shotgun Didn't Win the West

We are a nation of rifle shooters. Typically the "blam, blam, blam" that rang through the movie theater during Saturday afternoon matinees of our youth was not the sound of a twelve bore but rather the sound of a Winchester or a Colt. Occasionally some oaf would carry a scattergun, but rarely was he our hero. Usually the character who resorted to a shotgun was the protagonist's sidekick, a poor boob who lacked the nerves of steel and the eagle eye necessary to perform the feats of marksmanship that kept us riveted in our seats. Is it any wonder we prefer the rifleman image?

What was the first gun you fired? Most likely it was a BB gun or perhaps a .22 rifle. What were you taught? Hopefully, you were given basic safety instruction, but in terms of shooting technique, what were you coached to do? Put the front sight in the center of the peep or buckhorn rear sight and align the sights with the bull's-eye on your target. Once the sight picture is correct, hold everything steady and squeeze the trigger ever so carefully. Well, something like that anyway; hopefully, your mentor was more knowledgeable about rifle technique than I. If you missed your target, you tried again and were careful to hold everything steadier and to align your sights more precisely. Through practice and your coach's encouragement you eventually learned to hold your rifle steady and to aim with precision. This early training leaves an indelible mark on most of us. We are under its influence all our shooting lives, whether we are conscious of its influence or not. We seem to have a strong inclination to apply this rifle training to all subsequent shooting situations. Even those students who have never fired a gun of any type prior to coming to one of our shotgunning classes generally exhibit a predisposition to aim.

There is an obvious difference between the demands of most rifle shooting and the demands of most shotgunning. Typically, rifle shooters need more precision than do shotgunners. Rifle shooters shoot a single projectile and, generally speaking, are shooting at much longer range. This demand for precise bullet placement requires that rifle shooters aim the shot. Shotgunners fire a charge of shot that will compensate for a degree of imprecision, but they are almost invariably trying to hit a fast-moving target. I don't believe most experienced shooters would argue that the same techniques should be used with both rifle and shotgun. Most recognize that a shotgun should be pointed and that a rifle should be aimed. The difference between pointing and aiming is in the amount of visual attention given to the gun. When aiming a rifle the shooter tries to be conscious of the barrel-target relationship. The target is in most instances stationary, and taking time to make a precise alignment allows the shooter to attain the accuracy demanded in most situations. When pointing a shotgun, our focus should be exclusively on our target. The shooter relies on a properly mounted gun to ensure a natural alignment of the barrel with the line of sight. This technique is not as precise as aiming but is better suited to keeping up with a fast-moving target. As apparent as the differences in technique may be when we are discussing the topic, those differences seem to blur when the shooter steps to the firing line. Most people exhibit a natural predisposition to aim, whether they are using a rifle or a shotgun.

We must segregate our wingshooting techniques from our rifle and pistol techniques first and foremost. Within the framework of shotgunning we must also be careful to keep things segregated. The tools and techniques appropriate to the trap field may not work so well on the skeet field or in the dove field. Some readers may think this is obvious, and I couldn't agree more. Then why is it that we find shooters trying to use their trap or skeet techniques or equipment in the game field? The style of shooting and the equipment should be tailored to the shooting environment. This book is written for the field shotgunner. I make no claim regarding the applicability of the technique or tools to any other shooting situation.

My point is a simple one. Rifle, pistol, trap, skeet, and wing-shooting in the field are different and require different styles of shooting. I am waving the banner of the field gunner because it is my impression that most of what has been written in this country about shotgunning has not drawn these distinctions clearly enough. You may be an Olympic gold medal–winner in cross-country skiing, but if you apply your skinny little skis and your cross-country kick-and-glide technique to ski jumping or downhill, you could seriously hurt yourself. Yet, all three activities are surely skiing. Unfortunately, many shotgunners seem oblivious to the differences in their sport. The difference that many wingshooters fail to recognize is the difference between the technique used in clay target competitions such as trap or skeet and the technique best suited to most field shooting situations. I will enumerate what I feel are the principal differences between field and clay target shooting in chapter 2.

Clay Target Versus Field Shooting

Predictability is the principal difference between clay target and field shooting. The degree of predictability varies between the different clay target games, but none can replicate the spontaneity of field shooting. In the field we never know when a bird will flush or swing in over our decoys. Even with the best of dog work, events are never totally predictable. We don't know what the speed, range, or angle of flight will be or when any, or all, of these may change. Because of the spontaneity of field shooting, we are generally forced to mount our gun coincident with the flight of the bird. Preshouldering the gun is generally not an option.

In the majority of clay target situations the shooter determines when the target will be launched and knows what the flight pattern of the target will be. Preshouldering the gun is easily accomplished, and if our goal is to break as many targets as possible, it makes sense. There certainly is no right or wrong, in an absolute sense, as to whether you do your shotgunning with a preshouldered gun or with a "low-gun" starting position. But it does have an impact on your style of shooting and on how applicable that style will be to other shooting situations. I am not being judgmental; my only point is that very different techniques or styles are used for preshouldered clay target competition and for field shooting.

In no manner am I disparaging clay target competitions, whether they are trap, skeet, sporting clays, or any other. They are all challenging, fun to shoot, and have a loyal following. Neither am I detracting from the talents of competitive clay target shooters. On the contrary, I am respectful of their skill and consistency, particularly under the pressures of competition. The level of concentration and focus required is beyond me, and to maintain that level through hundreds of targets is more than I can fathom. Because of these demands a premium is put on consistency. To ensure that the playing field is level for all competitors, there must be a repetition of target presentation. To be competitive, clay target shooters need a system that will be consistent within the parameters of the game. They need consistency where field shooters need flexibility. Field shooters never know what the next shot will be. Their system must be simple and adaptable.

In many instances clay target enthusiasts can practice the shots they will encounter in the next competition. Particularly if shooting with a preshouldered gun, we can develop a series of sight pictures that solves each of the shot presentations. That is to say, we look for a particular barrel-target relationship on each shot. Clay target shooters can practice specific shots because of the nature of the game. Field shooters never know what the next shot will be, so their practice must be directed toward developing a style that will adapt itself to any shot. The necessity of mounting the gun coincident with the flight of the bird and the lack of foreknowledge of the bird's flight path dictate a difference in styles. I reiterate: I am not being judgmental. One system is not universally superior to the other. Each system is tailored to the demands of the game that it evolved around. Just don't make the all-too-common mistake of failing to recognize the differences and trying to apply a technique when it is not applicable.

Field gunners need a system that is simple, one that will allow them to successfully coordinate many variables in a split second. They need a technique that will utilize to full advantage the capabilities of eye and hand and require a minimum of thought. An accomplished field shooter relies on natural eye-hand coordination and a gun-mounting technique, or swing, that has been practiced to develop muscle memory. There should be no conscious alignment or aiming in the system. The Churchill, or instinctive, system is well suited to the field. It is simple and versatile. It relies on natural eye-hand coordination. At the core of the system is one well-founded assumption: We all have the ability to point. We can look at an object and point it out without having to think about the process. We do not have to sight along our outstretched finger and look at the relationship of the finger to the object and home in on it, so to speak. We are not visually conscious of the finger as we point. Rather, we keep our eyes fixed on the object we wish to bring attention to, and the finger is brought into proper alignment without any conscious thought process.

Eye-hand coordination allows us to hit a golf ball or a tennis ball or a baseball. We rely on that coordination constantly, yet in most instances we are unaware of it. It is one of the gifts that we take for granted. Not everyone is blessed with the same degree of eye-hand skills, but everyone can improve eye-hand skills with practice. The Churchill system relies on our native eye-hand skills. It is the only shooting technique I am aware of that unequivocally instructs shooters not to look at the gun. Most shooters I have worked with seem predisposed to mistrust their natural pointing abilities and feel the necessity to double-check the alignment at the last second. They might make the initial alignment instinctively, but just prior to pulling the trigger they want to look down to the gun to check the barrel-target relationship. This propensity to aim may be a product of rifle training, or it may just be instinctual. Whatever its roots may be, this propensity to aim is at the heart of many of the problems experienced by shooters in the field. The problem with aiming in most field situations is that it diverts the shooter's attention from the bird. A flight plan has not been prefiled for us, as it has in most clay target games. Aiming tends to slow the shooter's response to the trigger because it slows the swing. Aiming is too complex a system for most field shooting situations. If we are shooting clay targets that are flying a predetermined path, the instinct to aim may be less problematic. In all likelihood, we have practiced this shot and have familiarized ourselves with the flight path of the target.

The most important rule in field shooting is to keep your eye on the bird—not on the barrel. The eye is not capable of keeping the bird and the barrel both in sharp focus. When the eye is focused on the target at typical shotgun range, twenty-five to thirty yards, the bead on the barrel, twenty-five to thirty inches away, is a hazy blur. If we aim, visual attention will shift to the barrel, the target will become the blurred image, and we momentarily will lose track of its position. As with a camera lens, the eye's depth of field is limited. We do not have sufficient depth of field to keep both bird and barrel sharply focused. The eye is similar to a camera lens in another regard: Changes in focus are not made instantaneously. Just as a moment is required to rotate the barrel of the camera lens to adjust the focus, the eye requires a moment to shift its focus. What usually happens when shooters aim (rather than point) at a moving target is that their attention shifts from target to barrel just as they are ready to pull the trigger. When shooters try to clear up the fuzzy image of their gun, they will generally slow, or stop, their swing. If you are trying to focus on an object, you will intuitively hold it still; it is easier to see if it is not moving. This attempt to be too precise gets many wingshooters into trouble.

Try pointing at a blackbird or a pigeon as it flies overhead. As you make the point, you won't be visually conscious of your hand. Now double-check yourself by looking down at your finger and see if the alignment is correct. When you look back to the bird you'll find that your finger has fallen behind. It's the same with a shotgun. The problem with this visual confirmation, or aim, in field shooting is that it distracts your eye from a moving object that has no set pattern. As we look down to the gun and attempt to clarify the fuzzy image of the barrel, we lose track of the bird and usually slow or stop our swing. Field gunners must develop confidence in their instinctive ability to point, to trust their natural eye-hand coordination. Unfortunately, this inclination to look down at the last second is strong in many shooters. I have used a golf analogy that has seemed helpful to many students. I am not a golfer, but even I understand that if you cannot resist the natural inclination to look up before the club head strikes the ball, you will have little success. We want to see that ball sailing down the fairway, but we have to train ourselves not to look up prematurely. The urge to look down at the gun just prior to pulling the trigger is equally strong, but we must train ourselves to resist. I believe all eye-hand sports have this issue in common; we cannot allow ourselves to break our visual lock on the object we are trying to hit. The old adage "Keep your eye on the ball" may be well worn, but it is at the core of all eye-hand activities. Wingshooting is no exception.

Students frequently ask, "Where did I miss that target?" or "I was over that one, wasn't I?" They want to know if they were high, low, left, or right on every shot. Their curiosity is understandable, but I usually avoid answering their question even if I am sure where the miss occurred. Where the miss occurred is usually traceable to an error in technique. As a field shooter you should always be focused on form; don't worry about where you missed; find out *why* you missed. Field shooters who are fixated on where they miss each bird are missing a much more important issue. These shooters are still thinking in terms of aim. They have not made the mental transition; they are still thinking of wingshooting as an engineering problem, as opposed to an eye-hand sport with a technique or form. Shooters who remain fixated on where they are missing every shot are still thinking in terms of learning individual shots. The field shooter's world has too many variables to be categorized into specific shots. Successful field shooters have not memorized the solution to individual shots. They don't maintain a catalog of sight pictures in their heads and attempt to apply a specific solution to each shot.

I generally use another golf analogy to help students clear this mental hurdle. I suggest that if they were a golfer and had a problem with a bad slice they would probably go to their club pro for help. The pro would undoubtedly ask to see them hit several shots on the practice range. Presumably these golfers would hit a few shots, most of which would land well right of the point of aim (my hypothetical golfers are right-handed). If your golf pro said that he had an easy fix and suggested that if you merely adjust your stance such that your point of aim is forty or fifty degrees left of the fairway, you might occasionally keep a ball in play, you probably would find this advice unprofessional. Golfers understand that they must find and correct the error in their swing if they are to improve their game and lower their scores. They do not think in terms of making aiming corrections; rather, they think in terms of improving their swing. Why are golfers so much more perceptive than shotgunners, particularly when many of the students we coach are also avid golfers?

The answer lies in their perceptions of the two activities. They think of golf as a sport that has a form or style that is recognizable. They understand that eye-hand coordination plays an important role in their sport, but they also appreciate the necessity of developing a proper swing. They realize that when they hit a good shot it is not just because they aimed in the right direction. They understand that a well-made shot is the product of a well-executed swing. As a matter of course, when they go to a professional for help, they are hoping to improve their swing. They learned early on the necessity of keeping their eye on the ball; that concept is rudimentary for every golfer. Why is their approach sophisticated and insightful with regard to golf, but so naïve and lacking in insight with regard to wingshooting? They typically are still thinking of wingshooting as a simple matter of aiming. They do not understand that wingshooters in the field who consistently make clean kills are successful because they are executing their swing well. They have developed a form, or style, that incorporates numerous elements, from stance to gun mount to timing and visual concentration, all of which contribute to their well-made shot. They are successful because they have good technique in the same way good golfers are successful because they have a good technique. Have you ever heard Tiger Woods described as a golfer who aims really well?

If your goal is to improve your wingshooting skills in the field, be mindful of all the elements that contribute to a well-made shot in the field. Make your practice sessions as productive as you can by simulating field conditions as closely as possible. If all your practice sessions with clay targets involve shooting with a preshouldered gun, you can't expect this practice to produce the optimum benefit to your field technique. Again, I want to make clear that I am not being judgmental; there is nothing inherently good or bad, right or wrong, when it comes to shooting preshouldered versus "low-gun." But it does have a profound effect on the form, or technique, that we will develop as a shotgunner.

Sporting clays was in its infancy in the United States twenty-odd years ago, when this book was first published. The popularity of sporting clays is one of the factors prompting my revision of the original text. Not that shotgunning has changed because of sporting clays. What a wingshooter must do to be consistently successful in the field has not changed. But sporting clays has seemed to revive interest in shotgunning in general. The new clay target format found an enthusiastic group of shooters whose members were looking for something other than traditional skeet or trap. The format was billed as golf with a shotgun. Target presentations are more varied than in the older clay target games, but there is an element of repetition. Typically the same pair of targets is shot several times at each station, and the shooter can ask to see a pair of targets before attempting to shoot the station. The format offers an interesting amalgam of the older clay target games and some of the aspects of field shooting. One of its great virtues from the perspective of the field shooter looking for a place to practice is that it has generally been shot from the low-gun starting position. I understand that some shooters are now opting to use the preshouldered style on sporting clays courses. I am not passing judgment on how you choose to shoot. But if your goal is to become the best field shooter possible, shooting sporting clays from the low-gun position will be better practice.

Basic Technique   3

All shooters seem to be looking for the one trick that will ensure that they will never miss again. And the more naïve shooters are, the more likely they are to be looking for the bit of magic that will make them a great shot. Why is it that perfectly intelligent people have such totally unrealistic expectations when it comes to shooting? There are no magic formulas. To be a successful shooter, you must understand the basic technique and practice enough to develop and maintain proper muscle memory and timing.

Learning to be a good field shooter is like learning to play golf. First you must learn the swing. Before you can hope to be successful you must understand the principles involved and have a mental image of what a good swing looks like. Learning this is relatively easy for golfers. Many good books are available to help, and golfers can easily enlist the aid of a pro. But relatively little has been written about the shotgun swing as it pertains to the field. Numerous books discuss hunting strategies or deal with the relative merits of various loads or the degrees of choke best suited to various conditions. Likewise, books to help the dedicated clay target shooter are relatively easy to find. But relatively few books deal with shooting technique as it pertains to the field.

In this chapter I will describe what I believe are the components of a good shotgun swing. As in all sports, there is room for individuality. If you analyzed the swings of the top ten money winners on the PGA tour, you would find they all have their own styles. You would also find that they have many things in common. The same is true of wingshooters. They may all have their own styles, but they also have many common denominators. I have been using the term *swing*, but *gun mount* is perhaps more accurate and descriptive of the shotgunner's motion. For the field shooter, gun mount and swing combine to become one continuous motion. Skeet shooters and trapshooters typically mount their gun as a preliminary action, so their swing becomes a separate movement. I will discuss gun mount and swing as one because I believe they should be for the field gunner.

The Churchill system is based on one well-founded assumption: We are all born with a natural ability to point. Reduced to its basic elements, the system requires shooters to use a properly fit gun, to use correct gun-mounting technique or a good swing, and to keep their eye on the bird. The necessity of keeping your eye on the bird has already been discussed. Gun fit will be considered in chapter 4. Let's look at the gun mount, or swing.

STANCE

Let's begin our discussion with the feet and work up. Accomplished wingshooters keep their feet as close together as possible while maintaining good balance. If the footing is firm and the terrain relatively level, the heels should be quite close together.

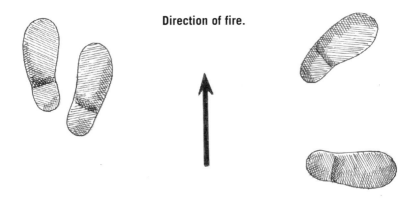

Direction of fire.

Correct narrow stance.   Wide rifle-style stance.

The feet should always be placed so that the distance between them is less than the breadth of the shooter's shoulders. If you are a right-handed shooter, the left foot should be pointed in the anticipated direction of fire and slightly ahead of the right. The right foot should be toed out slightly. Throughout this discussion I will adopt the view of a right-handed shooter. If you are left-handed, just reverse my right and left designations. If we think in terms of a clock face, the left foot would be on twelve o'clock, while the right would be on two o'clock. If the feet were brought together, the ball of the right foot would meet the arch of the left.

It is important to keep the shoulders and hips square to the direction of fire. Your belly button should be pointing in the same direction as the gun. Your initial stance should have you facing in the anticipated direction of fire. If the target swings right or left, you must be able to turn your entire body in order to remain square with the target. By maintaining this orientation to the target, you will facilitate the instinctive point response. Your left hand will be best able to respond to the direction from the eye and naturally align your gun with your line of vision. A narrow stance will allow you to pivot freely and keep your hips and shoulders moving together. Proper footwork will allow you to swing your gun through a 180-degree arc without losing your

A narrow stance will allow a shooter to pivot freely and keep the shoulders level and head erect.

A wide stance will force a shooter to lean and drop his head.

balance or moving your feet. Pivoting on a narrow base will help you keep your shoulders level and your head steady as you turn. It is most important for a shooter to minimize head motion. If your eye remains steady, it is relatively easy for you to instinctively point out your target. If your head and eye are moving as you point, the formula for alignment becomes complicated. Try it; consciously move your head to the side as you attempt to point at an object. Tough, isn't it? Now, hold your head steady and point. Much easier, isn't it?

Wingshooting is by no means unique in this regard. Steadying the head makes any eye-hand activity easier. Watch good golfers or good baseball batters as they swing; better yet, look at sequential photographs of the swings of either. You will see an absolute minimum of head motion. When you swing a shotgun, the part of your anatomy farthest from your head has a tremendous effect on how steady you hold it. The position of your feet will determine, to a large extent, the stability of your head during the swing.

Most shooters I have worked with are inclined to spread their feet too far apart. A wide stance increases the tendency to lean as shooters swing on a target. With the feet spread apart it is nearly impossible to pivot; one lacks the narrow base necessary to do so. The wide stance prevents the hips and shoulders from moving together. The wide base holds the hips in a nearly fixed position. As the shooter tries to swing right or left, the upper body begins to lean and pulls the head down. Typically, the shoulder in the direction that the shooter is turning will drop. That is, if the shooter is attempting a left-to-right crossing shot, his right shoulder will drop as he turns. As his right shoulder drops, his head will be pulled down with it. Crossing targets are often missed low and behind, a miss that can often be attributed to a stance that is so wide that it makes the shooter lean over as he tries to swing on the target.

The U.S. shooter's predisposition toward a wide stance is yet another by-product of our rifle bias. Spreading your feet and dropping your shooting shoulder back are fine if your target is stationary. This stance gives good stability, but it is not flexible enough for something as dynamic as wingshooting. With the correct narrow stance, the hips and shoulders can move together. This pivoting motion allows shooters to keep their shoulders level and their head erect. This swing helps them keep their eye steady and makes their gun point more naturally.

READY POSITION

Whenever possible, a shooter should come to a ready, or alert, position prior to making the gun mount. If we have one standard starting position, we can more easily develop and consistently execute our gun mount. If we are to become accomplished field shots, we must develop consistency in our gun mount. Our gun must meet the cheek and shoulder properly to ensure a natural alignment of the barrel with the line of vision. Use of a standardized starting position will make it easier to develop the muscle memory necessary to ensure consistency.

Most shotgunners are oblivious to their starting position. After they fire a shot, they would be hard pressed to tell you what position their gun was in when they swung into action. As they begin one shot the gun is over the shoulder; on the next shot the gun might be held at port arms; and on the third shot it might be pointing straight up. This inconsistency in initial gun position needlessly complicates the gun mount. The movement required to bring the gun from over the shoulder to a proper shooting position is significantly different from the movement required to move the gun from port arms to shooting position. Why learn several different gun mounts? If we standardize our initial position, we need to learn just one pattern of movement. Everything we do to simplify the task of mounting the gun is a plus.

As field gunners we do not enjoy much control over our environment. We cannot dictate when a shot will occur. We cannot maintain one gun attitude throughout a long day in the field. I am not suggesting we walk all day with our gun held at the ready, or alert, position. Carry your gun in a comfortable and safe position, as you are accustomed to doing. When your dog goes on point, and you are expecting the birds to break, adopt your standard ready, or alert, position. Even if you manage to hold that position for only a fraction of a second, you have gotten the job done.

Some types of shooting lend themselves better to the ready position than do others. It is certainly easier to use a standard ready position on a European-style driven shoot than on a walk-up shoot. Standardizing your starting position is more difficult when shooting quail or ruffed grouse in heavy cover, but if you can discipline yourself to ready the gun momentarily before making the move to shoulder, you will be a better shot. The perception of most shooters is that they need to be quicker than the situation actually demands. We perceive that we have less time to make our shot than we actually have. If we can train ourselves to bring the gun to the ready for even a split second, our gun mount will be more consistent.

Many students describe to me in great detail hunting situations in which adopting a ready position would be extremely difficult. I never argue because I agree. In many situations adopting a standard ready position is difficult at best. Do what you can. Just because the technique is difficult to adopt in some situations is not justification for scrapping it. In many cases coming to the ready is easy, and doing so will improve your gun mount and swing, no matter what degree of difficulty you incur in getting there. What we are trying to do is simplify the gun mount. No matter how tough it may be for you to use a ready position, doing so will make everything easier from that point on. What happens after the ready position has been assumed is critical.

What is the best ready position? Shooters must hold the gun at a safe attitude and in a manner that will minimize the difficulty in bringing it to shoulder. The gun position should neither obstruct shooters' field of view nor distract visually from

A good ready or alert position.

their target. Lastly, the gun's preliminary position should accentuate shooters' natural pointing instinct during the gun mount. The illustration on page 21 shows the position that I suggest to students. The heel of the stock should be tucked just under the shooting arm and drawn up to the underarm. The muzzles should be at eye level and right in front of the shooter's nose. About two inches of the stock should be caught under the arm. If the stock is pulled farther back under the arm, the gun mount motion is unnecessarily complicated. If too little stock is under the arm, the stock may be pulled into position on the cheek

The muzzles should be held directly in front of the shooter in the ready position.

before the lead hand has had a chance to naturally point the barrels at the target.

The Churchill system is based on our natural ability to point. Thus, we must use a gun mount that will accentuate our natural pointing instincts. Point at something; now carefully analyze what you did. Your hand with outstretched finger did not come straight up in front of your eye. You pushed your hand out more than you raised it. This is what we must do with our shotgun if we are to best utilize our instincts. By burying a couple of inches of the stock under our arm, we are unable to lift the stock

A good ready position will help a shooter mount the gun to shoulder properly.

straight up to our cheek. We are forced to push the gun forward as we begin the gun mount. As we push the gun forward, we approximate the natural point gesture.

The lead hand (left hand for a right-handed shooter) does the pointing and should provide direction to the gun mount. The gun mount should be more push than lift. The lead hand should do most of the work of moving the gun from the ready position to the firing position. We want to position the lead hand on the forestock to accentuate the instinctive point gesture. Point at something again; now look at the position of your hand and arm. Your hand is well out in front of your face, and your arm is nearly extended. That is the natural pointing attitude, and that is where your lead hand should be when the gun is shouldered. Carefully place your gun on your shoulder so that the heel of the stock is even with the top of your shoulder. Now put your left hand out in

The gun should not be slung across the chest in the ready position

a natural pointing attitude and place the forestock in your left hand. Slip the gun off your shoulder and pull the heel of the stock back under the armpit a couple of inches. Lower the muzzles to eye level and position them squarely in front of your face. There you have it: an efficient ready position. From this starting point you can push the gun forward and up to the shoulder with an economy of motion that utilizes your natural pointing instincts.

Be careful that your ready position does not sling the gun across your chest. It is important that the muzzles be in front of your nose, not in front of your left shoulder (presuming you are a right-handed shooter). If the gun is allowed to lie across your chest, it will give you a tendency to mount the gun out on your arm. This tendency will make you shoot across your line of vision. A right-hander will be inclined to shoot left. In the ready position the gun should be held as close as possible to ninety de-

If the gun is held across the chest in the ready position, the gun will very likely be mounted to the arm rather than the shoulder.

grees to the line of the shoulders. This positioning will help keep the gun on the shoulder as the mount is made and minimize the tendency to shoot across the line of vision.

The fingers of the lead hand must be spread out enough to prevent them from wrapping over the top of the barrels. We want an unobstructed line of sight directly to our target. This positioning becomes an issue if we are shooting a side-by-side with a splinter forestock. If we are shooting an over-under, or most any other type of shotgun, there is sufficient depth in the forestock to prevent the fingers of our lead hand from obstructing our view of the target. The gun should be held firmly but not with a white-knuckle grip. The fingers of the trigger hand should wrap around the wrist of the stock with the trigger finger outstretched and lying along the side of the trigger guard. Never place your finger on the trigger in the ready position. The trigger finger should not contact the trigger until the instant when the gun is fired. The trigger should be pulled with the end of the index finger. Do not wrap your finger around the trigger so that the first knuckle is

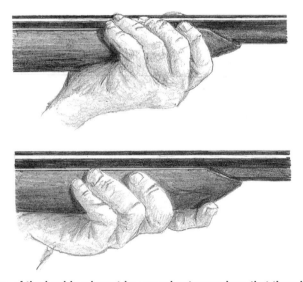

The fingers of the lead hand must be spread out enough so that they do not wrap over the top of the barrels.

The trigger finger should lie alongside the trigger guard at the ready.

The trigger should be pulled with the very end of the index finger.

Do not wrap your finger around the trigger.

The thumb should push across a top tang safety with a diagonal motion. The thumb should wrap around the stock after the safety has been disengaged.

If using a trigger guard safety, the tip of the index finger should rest on the safety in the ready position.

past the trigger. You have the best feel for the trigger when you pull it with the fleshy tip of your finger.

If you are using a breaking gun or any gun with a top tang safety, the thumb of your trigger hand should be on the safety. Your thumb should push across the safety with a diagonal motion. A right-handed shooter pushes the thumb from right to left as it moves forward to disengage the safety. The thumb continues that motion after the safety has been disengaged so that the thumb ends up being wrapped around the wrist of the stock. Do not leave your thumb on top of the safety if you are shooting a breaking gun with a top lever. If your thumb is left on top of the safety, recoil can jam your thumb into the back of the lever, giving you an unforgettably sore thumb. If your gun is equipped with a trigger guard safety, you should rest the tip of your trigger finger on the safety in the ready position. After you have pushed off the safety, your finger moves to the trigger.

No matter what style of safety you are using, as a field gunner you should strive to integrate disengagement of the safety into your gun-mount reflex. That is to say, you should not disengage the safety as a preliminary action. You should keep the safety engaged until you sight the bird and decide to fire. Only when you initiate the gun mount should you disengage the safety. When working with new shooters I typically allow them to disengage the safety after they have assumed the ready position. With the gun at the ready the muzzles are pointed in a safe direction, and disengagement of the safety does not create an undue hazard. As students develop confidence in their gun-mounting technique, I encourage them to integrate disengagement of the safety into the gun-mount process. With practice, muscle memory takes over the gun mount, and the motion becomes a reflex action. Ideally, disengagement of the safety becomes part of that reflex pattern of movement.

TIMING AND MOTION

You are at the ready, and a bird flushes. Now what? The first thing a shooter must do is make visual contact with the target. Don't try to shoot it until you see it. This rule may sound ridiculously obvious, but believe me, most shooters are inclined instinctively to bring their gun fully to shoulder before they are visually locked onto their target. I have watched shooters raise their gun to shoulder and point it in a direction that had no relation to the flight of the bird. Their explanation is always, "I thought it was going over there." Field shooting should be based on natural eye-hand coordination; we need to allow our eye and hand to work together instinctively. The circuitry should be directly from eye to hand, and if we overthink the shot, we will probably miss.

What makes shooters raise their gun to shoulder before they have seen the target? They are overanxious; they allow themselves to react to the sound of the bird flushing or the sound of the trap launching the clay target. If we allow ourselves to mount our gun before our eye has locked on our target, we have thrown away our natural eye-hand point capability. If we allow ourselves to raise the gun fully to shoulder before our eye is on the target, we are trying to locate the bird with the gun barrels right in the middle of our field of vision. It is difficult not to be distracted by them. We must train ourselves not to mount the gun until we see our target. Don't allow yourself to mount the gun because you heard the bird flushing. Unfortunately this is what most shooters instinctively are inclined to do. It takes a conscious effort to suppress the instinct to snap the gun to shoulder at the first sound of the bird taking flight.

Experienced field shooters have trained themselves to see the bird before they bring their gun to shoulder. In most instances your ear certainly helps establish the initial bearing, but the gun mount is never completed until the bird is seen. It is during that moment when the bird is heard but not yet seen that seasoned field shooters will come to the ready position. They will also instinctively turn their body to face the direction the bird is flying. This initial alignment is often done almost exclusively by ear. The key is that the gun is not brought to shoulder until the eye is locked on the target. We cannot possibly use our pointing instincts to best advantage if we don't have our eye locked on the bird as we make our gun mount.

Not only must we train ourselves to see the bird before we shoulder our gun, but also we must train ourselves to see detail on our target. If we can train our eye to identify a detail on the target, we will enhance the likelihood of maintaining our visual lock on the bird. Just like golfers who focus on one dimple on the ball to help themselves maintain their concentration and prevent themselves from looking up prematurely, we can gain a similar edge in concentration if we can identify a detail on our target. Train yourself to look for the bird's head. Don't allow yourself to see just a blur of wings; discipline yourself to find a detail. Even when you are not shooting, make it a habit to look at the head of every bird you see.

Slow Down

The hand is quicker than the eye. Give your eye a chance to see the bird. All too often I have watched shooters snap their gun to shoulder with a motion similar to that of a flyweight boxer throwing a jab. Following the blur that was their gun mount, shooters typically slam on the brakes. Next they execute a series of jerks and stops with a panicked urgency before they finally yank the trigger. This "hop and stop" technique is rarely successful. Wingshooters need to develop a fluid motion as they execute their gun mount. A gun that starts quickly will usually stop quickly. If you can train yourself to start your gun moving slowly, you will be well on your way to developing a smooth, continuous swing. The gun mount must be a controlled, coordinated movement. The faster we try to move, the greater the difficulty we incur in controlling our movement and in accomplishing a mount that brings the gun into proper position. Start slowly and allow the gun to accelerate through the mount and to swing to whatever degree is necessary to smoothly flow through the bird as you fire. Unfortunately, most people, by nature, seem inclined toward the "hop and stop" sort of motion and timing. You must galvanize yourself and resist this instinct to overreact to the target. Initially it will require a concerted effort to slow yourself down. But with practice you will learn to mount your gun with a pace that is appropriate to the speed of the bird.

Novice shooters typically want to get their gun to shoulder as quickly as possible and then take their time as they sight down the barrel and try to aim. Although this timing seems to be instinctive for the majority of students, they must not allow their instincts to prevail. Wingshooters must learn to suppress their inclination to hurry the gun to shoulder. They must learn to allow sufficient time for their eye to lock onto the target at the beginning of the process. Likewise, they must learn to allow sufficient time to execute the gun mount so that it will be a fluid motion. But with the eye locked on and a smooth gun mount accomplished, they must also learn to shoot with confidence. Do not ride the target excessively once the gun mount is complete. The longer your gun stays on your shoulder, the more likely you are to be distracted by it.

Relax

You cannot move smoothly if your body is too tense. You must be visually sharp, but you cannot afford to allow this visual acuity to transform itself into a white-knuckle grip on your gun and a tensing of every muscle in your body. Again the similarity to other eye-hand activities is obvious. To be successful at any eye-hand activity, you must be able to bear down visually without tensing every muscle.

Most of us have a little too much neck to be automatically ideal shooting machines. If the head does not move forward, the eye is held too high above the line of the barrels.

Your stance is narrow, you have come to a good ready position, you have locked your eye onto the target, and you have turned to face squarely in the direction of fire. What next? The lead hand should push the gun into shooting position and simultaneously and instinctively point the target out. The trigger hand helps push the gun to shoulder, but the lead hand should do most of the work. The gun should slip out from under the arm and come up to meet the underside of the shooter's cheekbone. Head motion should be held to a minimum. Ideally, the head should remain perfectly steady, and the gun should come all the way up to meet the cheek. For all but a very few this is difficult to do. Most shooters have to drop their head slightly to attain the proper relationship between eye and barrel. If they hold their head perfectly still, the eye is positioned too far above the line of the barrel. This positioning will result in a tendency to shoot high. Most of us have a little too much neck to be anatomically ideal shotgunners.

The manner in which we move our heads is critical. The head should move ever so slightly forward. This motion lowers our eye with a minimum of adverse effect on our natural pointing

The manner in which the head moves is extremely critical. The head should move ever so slightly forward.

Do not tip the head to the side as the gun is mounted.

abilities. If a stock were designed to accommodate the length of our necks in an upright posture, we would have a degree of drop in the stock that would make recoil more unpleasant (see chapter 4 on gun fit). The compromise is to design a comfortable stock that will distribute the recoil in a manner that minimizes discomfort and requires a minimum of head motion. It is extremely important that the head motion not be lateral. Many new shooters tip their head to the side in an attempt to bring their eye into alignment with the barrel. This tendency adversely affects the natural ability to point accurately and makes recoil that is felt in the cheek most unpleasant.

The gun should slip out from under the arm, where it has been held at the ready, and move up and forward until the stock is in firm contact with the underside of the cheekbone. What about the shoulder? All but real novices realize that the shoulder and butt of the stock should be held firmly together to minimize the discomfort of recoil. If the stock is held away from the shoulder, the recoil will be much sharper. The key is to bring the shoulder forward to meet the buttstock rather than pull the gun back to the shoulder. The heel of the stock should slide up the face of the shoulder as the gun is mounted. As the gun comes into the cheek, the shoulder is rolled slightly forward in a sort of shrugging motion. This motion snugs the shoulder and stock together and minimizes the recoil. The heel of the stock should be level with the top of the shoulder. The butt of the stock should be just outside the high portion of the collarbone but not out on the arm. Proper placement on the shoulder is facilitated by use of a good ready position.

You should not pull the gun back to meet the shoulder because doing this has a tendency to interrupt the natural flow of the shot. Your weight should move with the target. If the initial stance is good, your weight will shift in the direction the target is moving, following the motion of the left hand and the gun. The lead hand will create a subtle shift of weight in the direction the target is moving. If the gun is pulled back to the shoulder, this natural weight shift is interrupted. As the gun is pulled back, there is an inclination to shift the weight back. Typically the weight will be

It is important that you lean into the shot. The weight should be on the balls of the feet.

shifted to the back foot. As your weight falls back, the muzzles will rise and in many instances cause you to miss over the bird. Rolling your shoulder into the gun accentuates the natural weight shift. In the ready position, your weight should be slightly forward, favoring the ball of the left foot (presuming a right-handed shooter). You want to lean into the shot. Your balance is improved, and you tend to be more agile when your weight is on the balls of the feet. Pulling the gun back to the shoulder tends to shift your weight back onto your heel and interrupt your swing.

The most important thing is to keep your eyes on the bird when you pull the trigger. You should never be visually focused on the gun. The gun should move in one smooth motion from the

Do not sit back on the heels as you shoot.

ready position to shoulder and cheek. Take the shot without hesitation. Do not look down at the gun to check the alignment. If there is any magic in the process, it is in our eye's intuitive ability to direct our hand straight to the object we are focused on without any conscious thought process. The key element in wingshooting, as in all eye-hand activities, is visual concentration. At the instant we pull the trigger our eye must be focused on the bird, not on the barrel.

It is important that you take the shot confidently as soon as the gun mount is completed. The longer you hold the gun in the fully shouldered position, the greater the likelihood that you will be visually distracted by the gun. Shoot with your first attempt. The gun mount and swing must be a smooth and fluid motion, but you must be decisive. When the gun mount is complete— shoot. Don't hold back and ride the target.

Many times I have watched shooters regress as they allow themselves to overthink a shot. Typically, when students are presented with a new shot—a target thrown at a different angle and range than those they had been practicing—I discuss with them the techniques they should be mindful of as they shoot. Usually I review the basic form: Be certain that your ready position is good, allow sufficient time for your eye to engage the target, make the gun mount a fluid motion, and shoot with confidence. In most instances students will respond to the new target presentation well and break the first couple of targets decisively. It is not uncommon for students to experience a little slump after their initial success and to miss several targets. They shoot their first few "new" targets instinctively, allowing their eye and hand to work together naturally. They have no preconceived notion of where the target is going. They are relaxed because this is something new, and if they miss, it is no big deal because this is new material. But after breaking the first few targets they begin to tense a little and overthink the shot.

A subtle change in timing is the tip-off to what is happening. Students shoot the first few targets as soon as the gun comes into the cheek and shoulder. As they begin to think too much and tense a bit their response to the trigger slows. There is no perceptible change in their motion, but they hold the gun on the shoulder just a little too long before taking the shot. Field gunners must train themselves to shoot confidently in one free-flowing motion. If they bring the gun to shoulder and then ride the bird as they attempt to double-check the alignment, they will lose the natural pointing instinct. The longer shooters ride the bird, the more likely their eye is to refocus on the barrel and the more likely they are to slow or stop their swing.

People often tell stories about gunners who were great shots. Some stories are more preposterous than others, but many have a common thread. Whether the great shot was in the marsh or the upland, he is frequently described as a shooter who "just pulled up and fired." This statement is made as further testimony to the fabled shot's stature; the implication is clearly, "Think how good he might have been if he took more time after shouldering the gun to make more certain of his alignment." In fact, it was the great shot's timing that contributed largely to his success. He was a veteran gunner and had developed the confidence to shoot in one fluid motion. Don't second-guess yourself. Move the gun smoothly to cheek and shoulder, keep your eye on the bird, and shoot with confidence.

The concept of getting the gun and body moving with the target before the gun is fully mounted is an important one. The swing and the gun mount are integrated. Unfortunately, most shooters seem naturally inclined to segregate the gun mount and the swing. They want to mount the gun fully to cheek and shoulder before starting to move, or swing, with the bird. This tendency, like many of our shotgunning problems, may be traceable to our early rifle training. The rifleman mounts his gun and

then aligns his sights. These two motions are distinct opera-
tions. A shotgunner on the skeet or trap field likewise segre-
gates gun mount from alignment. The field gunner must learn
to move with the target from the first moment they see it. They
actually start their swing before initiating the move to the
shoulder in some instances. Crossing shots are most demanding
in this regard. If shooters will learn to begin the lateral motion
necessary to keep them square with the target before they start
the gun up to shoulder, they will find crossing shots much easier. If they turn their shoulders and hips to keep themselves facing the bird as they mount the gun, they will have a natural
momentum to their swing. We depend on this natural momentum to keep us moving through our target. The question of lead
will be addressed in chapter 6. For now suffice it to say that if
we can learn to integrate our swing and gun mount, everything
will flow more naturally.

Gun Fit 4

T he Churchill system requires the use of a properly fit gun. The gun should be designed so that if it is properly positioned on the cheek and shoulder it will point exactly where the shooter is looking. The line of the barrels and the shooter's line of vision will naturally coincide if the gun is properly fit and if the gun mount is properly executed. We presume that the shooter has sufficient eye-hand coordination to point accurately. We further presume that the shooter will practice the gun-mounting motion until that motion is consistently correct. Let's consider what constitutes a properly fit gun.

A shotgun should be designed so that the shooter's eye will naturally align with the barrel. The size and shape of the stock should be determined by the physique of the shooter. Field shooting dictates that the gun be brought to shoulder and cheek with one smooth motion and that the shot be taken without hesitation. There is no time to adjust the gun on the shoulder and cheek to ensure that the eye is properly aligned. The stock should therefore be proportioned to the shooter. One size does not fit all, but, unfortunately, most guns are sold with only one size of stock. This fact is an unfortunate but unavoidable outgrowth of mass-produced guns. Firearms manufacturers cannot afford to produce and warehouse stocks of several sizes. If they did, the price of their shotguns would increase dramatically. Firearms manufacturers produce one standard-size stock that they hope will fit their average customer. Their Mr. Average is about five-feet-nine, weighs in the neighborhood of 165 pounds, and wears a size 40 regular suit. If this description sounds familiar, you may be one of those lucky people who can pick up most standard-stock shotguns and shoot them quite well. The further you are from this average in regard to size, the greater the likelihood you will benefit from buying a custom stock or from modifying a standard stock.

Proper alignment of the eye with the barrel is not the only consideration when fitting a stock. The stock must be designed to make the gun comfortable to shoot. The size and shape of the stock cannot affect the force of the recoil other than by the degree to which the stock adds weight, but the design of the stock can influence how comfortable the gun is to shoot. We want to minimize discomfort. The gun should be designed to distribute the recoil as evenly as possible.

How does a gun fitter go about achieving these ends of proper eye alignment and minimum recoil discomfort? When fitting a stock to a shooter a gun fitter should use a try gun. This is a gun that has an adjustable stock that can be tailored to the shooter. The illustration on page 43 gives the reader the nomenclature generally used to describe the parts of a gun stock and shows the measurements taken when a stock is fit.

By watching a shooter fire a try gun at a stationary target with a solid background, the gun fitter can tailor the stock to the shooter. The fitter watches as the shooter fires the try gun and can then look at the stationary target and see precisely where the shot charge struck. The target is placed on a large metal plate that has been painted white, thus allowing the fitter to assess the accuracy of the shot placement relative to the target. By adjusting the stock, the gun fitter adjusts the alignment of the shooter's eye relative to the barrel. If the gun is properly fit, and if the shooter executes the gun mount correctly, the line of the barrels and the shooter's line of vision will coincide.

In essence, the shotgunner's eye is used like the rear sight on a rifle. The gun fitter moves the shooter's eye relative to the barrel via physical changes to the size and shape of the stock, whereas the rifle shooter moves his or her sights. The fitter is trying to create a stock that if properly placed on the shoulder and cheek will place the shooter's aligning eye slightly above the line of the barrel, but centered left and right. We want a field gun to shoot just the slightest bit high at typical shotgun range. Such a gun will allow shooters to keep the bird in full view as they fire. If the fitter did not position the shooter's eye slightly above the

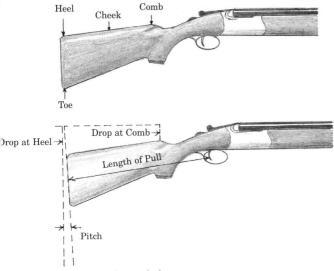

A properly fit gun is important.

line of the barrel, the shooter would be forced to bring the barrels directly between the eye and the bird and thereby partially obscure the target. Doing this tends to distract shooters and to

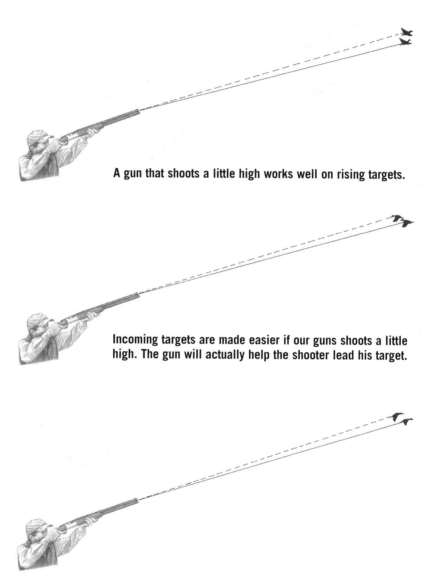

A gun that shoots a little high works well on rising targets.

Incoming targets are made easier if our guns shoots a little high. The gun will actually help the shooter lead his target.

An overhead bird that is going away is made more difficult to hit with a gun that shoots high. The occasions where a moderately high-shooting gun are a benefit seem to outweigh those where it is a hindrance.

break their visual lock on their target. The instinctive pointing gesture brings the pointer, whether it is our finger or our gun, just beneath the object at which we are looking. Try it—point at something. You will not obscure your view of the object you are pointing at by bringing your finger directly between your eye and the object. Typically you will bring your finger just beneath the object. Couple this with the fact that in most field situations a little rising lead is helpful, and the reason for designing our field gun to shoot a bit high becomes apparent. If we are walk-up shooting, typically birds flush and are rising as we shoot. A gun that shoots a little high will make this shot more natural. When we are pass shooting, birds many times are coming at us high overhead; the design of our stock now helps us naturally build a forward allowance into our mount. There certainly are occasions when the design of our stock may not be beneficial. Shooting a high bird that is flying away from us is one occasion. All in all, the stock designed to shoot a little high seems to be the most workable in the majority of field situations.

Our field gun should come to shoulder smoothly and easily, and it should distribute the recoil as evenly as possible to minimize discomfort. Let's consider each of the stock measurements and the impact it typically will have on our success.

LENGTH OF PULL

Most shooters are familiar with the measurement of length of pull. It is the distance from the rear of the buttstock to the face of the trigger. The length of pull significantly affects the shooter's performance. It determines to a large extent where the shooter's cheek will meet the stock. The greater the length of pull, the farther back on the stock the cheek will fall. I believe that most gun fitters would agree that the shooter's cheek should contact the stock just forward of the midpoint between comb and heel.

Length of pull is determined by the length of the shooter's arm, his general physique (slim or heavy), and the degree to which he thrusts his head forward as he mounts the gun. Generally speaking, the longer the arm, the slimmer the build, and the more the shooter pushes his head forward, the longer the stock should be. A shooter's stance will also influence the length of pull. Shooters who drop their shooting shoulder back will generally need a greater length of pull than will shooters who square their shoulder to their target. The old technique of placing the butt of the stock in the crook of the elbow and extending the trigger finger to determine the length of pull is crude at best. This technique considers only the length of the forearm. It does not take into account all the other factors that affect length of pull. By having the

The old technique to determine the length of pull: Place the buttstock in the crook of the elbow and extend the index finger to the trigger. This method is better than nothing, but is not really adequate.

The cheek should meet the stock just ahead of the midpoint between heel and comb.

shooter fire a try gun with an adjustable length of pull, the gun fitter can take into account all of the idiosyncrasies of the shooter's physique and style and arrive at a more accurate measurement.

Not only does length of pull affect the location of the cheek on the stock and thereby the relationship of eye to barrel, but also length of pull is the primary determinant of the gun's ease of mounting. If the stock is of the proper length the gun will come to shoulder smoothly with a minimum of seesawing. If the stock is too long, the gun will be difficult to shoulder without the heel of the stock catching under the shooter's armpit. The barrels will have a tendency to come up ahead of the stock, and the shooter will likely miss high.

A stock that is too long also may cause shooters to mount the buttstock out on their bicep rather than on their shoulder. Recoil is most unpleasant if the stock is on the arm rather than on the shoulder, and shooters will have a tendency to shoot

If the stock is too long it will be difficult to get the gun to shoulder without the heel catching under the shooter's arm.

A stock that is too long may cause a shooter to mount the butt on his bicep rather than into the shoulder.

across their line of vision. That is, a right-handed shooter will have a tendency to shoot left, and a left-hander will have a tendency to shoot to the right. A high bird that is coming directly overhead brings out this tendency to cross-fire in some shooters. A right-handed shooter will seldom miss this high incoming target on the right side. If the shooter makes a windage error, the error will generally be to the left. This tendency of the right-handed shooter to err to the left is usually traceable to a poor initial stance, a poor gun mount, or some combination of the two. And both of these mistakes may be linked to a stock that is too long.

If the stock is too short, the shooter's cheek will be placed too close to the comb of the stock. In the extreme case the thumb of the trigger hand may actually hit the shooter's nose when the gun is fired. A stock that is too short will tend to come to shoulder too fast. Many times the stock is cheeked before the barrels have been brought into position by the shooter's lead hand. A

If the stock is too short the thumb of the trigger hand may hit the shooter's nose when the gun is fired.

stock that is too short will accentuate the tendency that many shooters have of overpowering their gun mount with their trigger hand. This mistake will give the shooter a tendency to shoot low, or it may produce a two-part gun mount. By "two-part gun mount" I mean a gun mount that first positions the stock on the face but then requires a secondary motion to lift the barrels. This style of gun mount has little relation to the natural point gesture and may accentuate the tendency to aim. If the stock is the correct length, the entire gun mount process will happen more naturally. The gun should move out from under the arm and to shoulder and cheek in one smooth motion. Stock and barrels should move together without any seesaw motion.

Obviously we would prefer to shoot a gun that has a length of pull appropriate for us. But if we find ourselves forced to use a borrowed gun or one that does not have the correct length of pull for us, we can change the feel of the gun by changing the position of our lead hand. Normally we should place our lead hand far enough out on the forestock or barrels so that the weight of the gun will be evenly distributed between our hands. That is to say, we place our hands equidistant from the physical balance point of the gun. We must place our trigger hand for ease of operation of the trigger and the safety. Find the balance point of your gun and measure the distance from the balance point to the spot where your trigger hand grips the throat of your stock. If the buttstock is properly fit to you, your lead hand should be an equal distance forward of the balance point. If you are shooting a gun that feels too short, move your lead hand farther forward. Doing this obviously does not lengthen the stock, but it will give the gun a slightly longer feel. Conversely, if the gun in your hands feels too long, choke up a bit; that is, move your lead hand back slightly. This adjustment in the position of the lead hand cannot correct for a grossly ill-fit stock. There is no substitute for a stock of the correct length, but by adjusting your lead hand position you can compensate somewhat for the differences in length of pull created by different amounts of clothing.

DROP AT COMB

Drop at comb is the distance between the top of the barrels, or rib, and the top of the stock at the comb. You can easily measure this distance on your own gun by placing the gun upside down on a flat surface. With the top of the receiver and the barrels, or rib, flat against a tabletop or other level surface, measure the distance from the comb of the stock to the tabletop. Be careful that the bead, or beads, hangs over the edge of the table. If the bead rests on the tabletop, it will give a false measurement.

The combined effects of drop at comb and drop at heel determine the height of the eye relative to the rib, and the height of the eye relative to the rib is the principal determinant of how high the gun will tend to shoot. Generally speaking, the higher the shooter's eye, the higher the gun will tend to shoot. Of the two measurements, drop at comb is the more critical. Even small variations in this measurement will affect the height of the shotgun's patterning point. The shooter's cheek should contact the stock just a few inches behind the comb, and therefore changes as seemingly insignificant as one-eighth of an inch can have an

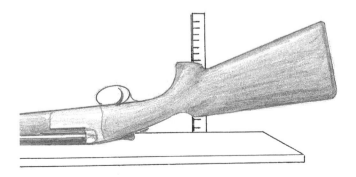

Measuring drop at comb

effect on the gun's patterning point. Shotguns intended for field use will commonly be produced with stocks that have one and one-half inch of drop at the comb. This distance will accommodate a large percentage of shooters. In my experience, the majority of field shooters can be accommodated by a drop at comb measurement from one and one-quarter to one and three-quarters inch. Trapshooters many times favor stocks that have little drop at the comb; the same holds true for live pigeon enthusiasts and some driven bird enthusiasts. The idiosyncrasies of these shooters' styles may be complemented by a gun with little drop. I am confining my discussion to the needs of the average field shooter, and I contend that a field shooter rarely benefits from less than one and one-quarter inch or more than one and three-quarters inch of drop at comb.

The amount of drop at comb required by a shooter is determined primarily by the distance from the underside of the

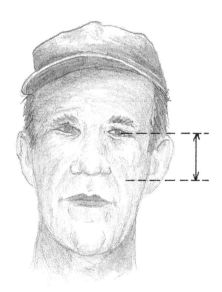

The amount of drop required is determined primarily by the distance from the underside of the shooter's cheekbone to the center of the eye.

shooter's cheekbone to the center of the eye. Typically a tall person with a long face will require more drop at comb than will a small, round-faced person. But no matter how large or small the shooter, there is not a tremendous variation in the distance between people's eyes and cheekbones. The amount of drop will also be affected by the shooter's gun mount. The more firmly the gun is brought into the cheek, the less the need for additional drop. If we increase the drop at comb, we lower the eye relative to the barrels; conversely, decreasing the drop raises the eye. If shooters using the instinctive, or Churchill, system increase drop and lower the eye, they will shoot lower. Decreasing drop has the opposite effect. When fitting a stock for field use we want the eye slightly above the line of the rib, or barrels.

DROP AT HEEL

Drop at heel is the distance between the top of the barrels, or rib, and the top of the stock at the heel. This measurement can be taken using the same procedure used for measuring drop at comb. As mentioned, the combined effect of drop at comb and drop at heel determines the height of the shooter's eye relative to the rib and thereby the inclination to shoot high or low. The principal determinants of the amount of drop at heel needed by shooters are the length of their neck and the degree to which they push their head forward as they mount their gun.

Shotguns designed for field use are commonly produced with stocks that have between two and one-quarter and two and one-half inches of drop at heel. This distance, combined with the typical drop at comb distance of one and one-half inch, will usually produce a workable stock for the gun manufacturer's average customer. Barring any unusual physical traits or any peculiarity in gun-mounting technique, these drop distances will be comfortable

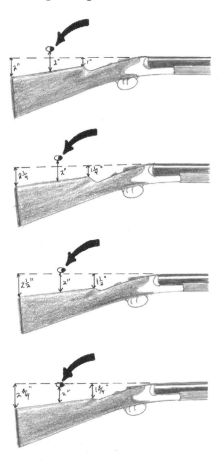

The combined effects of drop at comb and drop at heel determine the height of the eye relative to the rib or barrel.

and efficient for many shooters of average build. If shooters have a long neck and hold their head erect as they shoot, a little extra drop at heel may be beneficial. Conversely, if shooters have a short neck, or if they have a habit of lowering their head as they mount their gun, a little less drop at heel may be in order. In my experience a field shooter seldom benefits from a drop at heel of less than two inches or more than two and three-quarters inches. As with drop at comb, the variation in drop at heel is not great, but the impact that one-eighth or one-quarter of an inch can have is significant.

When fitting a stock, we are trying to place the shooter's

aligning eye behind the barrels in such a fashion that the gun will naturally point where the shooter is looking. We must also be mindful of the influence that drop will have on the distribution of recoil. In this regard, it is important to keep the drop at comb and the drop at heel in balance. That is, when fitting a customer with the try gun we must strive to minimize the difference between drop at comb and drop at heel. If the difference between drop at comb and drop at heel exceeds an inch, there is an increased likelihood that the gun will transfer more recoil to the cheek. The greater the difference between these two distances, the greater the apparent recoil to the cheek will be. The angle formed between the top of the stock and the barrels should be held to a minimum while still placing the shooter's eye in the proper position for alignment. A stock dimension that works well for many shooters of average build is one and five-eighths inch at the comb and two and one-quarter inches at the heel. This dimension places the eye at the same height relative to the barrels as the more common one and one-half inch at the comb and two

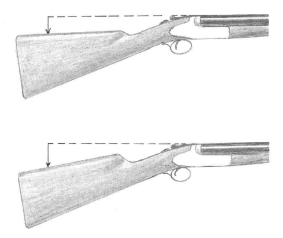

The greater the difference between drop at comb and drop at heel, the more the recoil will be felt in the cheek. The angle formed between the top of the stock and the barrels should be held to a minimum and still place the shooter's eye in the proper position.

and one-half inches at the heel. The advantage of lowering the comb and raising the heel slightly is to reduce the amount of recoil felt at the cheek.

The principle of reducing the angle formed between the top of the stock and the barrels can be taken to the extreme as far as the field shooter is concerned. Some shotguns designed for trapshooting are built with drop at comb and drop at heel that are identical, or nearly so, that is, one and one-half inch at both comb and heel. These guns are usually pleasant to shoot in terms of recoil felt at the cheek, but most field gunners would have a tendency to shoot over many birds with this stock. The trapshooter's technique has been tailored to harmonize with this type of stock. A trapshooter's environment is very controlled by field standards. Trapshooters almost invariably use a preshouldered gun, and their typical target presentation lends itself to this stock design. A field shooter using the instinctive pointing technique typically benefits from a little more drop at heel.

A field stock should have enough drop to place the eye just over the line of the barrels. For most people the distance from the center of the eye to the underside of the cheekbone is roughly two inches. It is no accident that a stock with one and one-half inch of drop at comb and two and one-half inches of drop at heel will have about two inches of drop at a point midway between. This distance is called "drop at cheek." Why not make the drop a uniform two inches from comb to heel and eliminate the angle that tends to increase recoil felt at the cheek? We build more drop into the heel than we do into the comb of our stock in order to place the gun more solidly on the shoulder. The shoulder is slightly lower than the cheek when we are in shooting position. A stock with a little extra drop at heel will come into the shoulder more naturally and better distribute recoil to the shoulder.

CAST

Cast is the distance that the stock is bent to the right or left relative to the barrels. The function of cast is to correct for any right or left alignment error. Just as drop is our elevation adjustment, cast is our windage adjustment. How much cast is required by a shooter is largely determined by the fullness of the

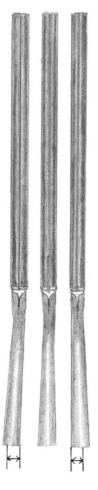

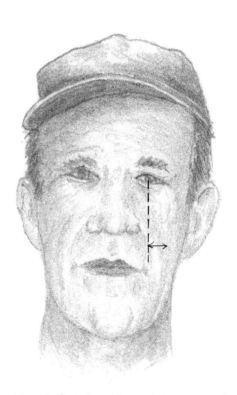

The principal determinant of the amount of cast required is the fullness of the face. People with broad faces may find that their eye is not directly above the spot where the stock contacts the cheek.

Cast is the distance the gun stock is bent to the right or left, relative to the barrels.

face and the width of the shoulders. When a shotgun is brought
to cheek and shoulder, it does not always fall into perfect alignment with the eye in a right-left orientation. Most shooters find
that their eye is slightly off-center. Right-handed shooters will
typically find that their eye is not directly in line with the barrel, but rather is off to the left when viewed from behind. Shooters with a broad, full face generally have the greatest problem
in this regard. Their eye is not directly above the spot where the
gun meets the cheek. Casting bends the stock away from the
face and allows the eye to attain a more direct alignment with
the barrels. A right-handed shooter is given *cast-off*: when the
gun is viewed from behind, the stock is offset to the right of the
line established by the barrels.

When a gun is brought to cheek it does not always fall into perfect alignment with the eye. Here the shooter's eye is positioned slightly to the right of the rib.

Casting bends the stock away from the shooter's face and allows his eye to move into proper alignment with the rib and barrels.

Cast not only compensates for the relationship between eye and cheekbone, but also makes the buttstock fall more naturally into the shoulder. The buttstock should come into the shoulder without contacting the high portion of the collarbone. Broad-shouldered shooters may discover that when the gun is so positioned it is angled slightly across their face. Looking at a right-handed shooter from behind we find that the gun is being pointed slightly to the left of the direction the shoulder is facing. By casting the stock we can achieve a more natural alignment of the gun with the direction of sight.

Most off-the-shelf shotguns are not cast because the manufacturer does not know whether the purchaser will be right-handed or left-handed. Nor does the manufacturer know how much cast would be required. Again we have the situation in which a manufacturer is producing one gun to fit the broadest range of shooters. The only logical option for the manufacturer who is producing off-the-shelf guns is not to cast the stocks. Given the dilemma faced by the major gun manufacturers, they do a remarkably good job with their "Mr. Average" approach.

PITCH

Pitch is the angle that the butt of the stock is cut relative to the barrels. If the butt of the stock forms a ninety-degree angle with the barrels, this angle is considered zero degrees of pitch. If the toe of the stock is cut back so that the angle formed between the barrels and the butt of the stock is less than ninety degrees, this angle is considered positive pitch. The pitch is measured in degrees from the right angle. A gun with plus four degrees of pitch would have a stock whose butt would form an angle of eighty-six degrees with the line of the barrels. A gun with minus four degrees of pitch would have a stock whose butt would form an angle of ninety-four degrees with the line of the barrels.

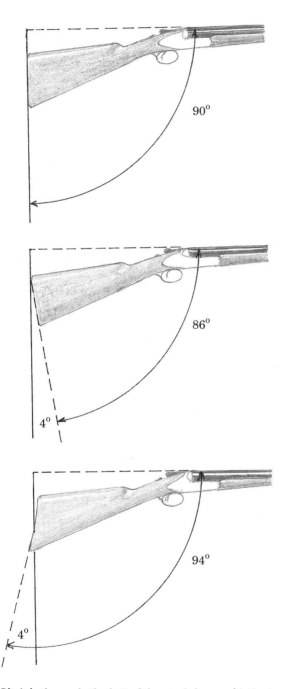

Pitch is the angle the butt of the stock forms with the barrels.

Most guns designed for field use are given a small amount of positive pitch. The stock designed for Mr. Average will usually have plus four degrees of pitch. Varying the pitch of a stock will affect how recoil is distributed on the shoulder and, to a lesser extent, affect how high or low the gun will tend to pattern. Let's consider the recoil aspect first. Most people will find that when they adopt a shooting position, the shoulder and chest area where the butt of the stock is placed does not form a ninety-degree angle with the barrels. The chest and pectoral muscles where the toe of the stock contacts the shooter's body are seldom directly beneath the shoulder area where the heel of the stock rests. The area where the toe of the stock meets the chest is usually a little forward of the shoulder. If a stock is cut with zero degrees pitch, the toe of the stock tends to push sharply into the chest, while the heel is held slightly away from the shoulder. The recoil is transferred primarily through the toe of the stock and digs into the chest. By cutting the stock with a modest amount of positive pitch we can make the buttstock conform more closely to the shape of the shoulder and chest. Doing this has the effect of distributing the recoil over the entire surface of the buttstock and makes the gun more comfortable to shoot. We have not affected the force with which the gun recoils; that is a function of the ammunition we use. But we have affected how the recoil is distributed. If the entire surface of the buttstock is in firm contact with the shoulder and chest, the recoil will be less apparent than if only a small part of the buttstock is transferring the energy to the shoulder.

The shape of the shoulder and chest will determine the amount of pitch required. A barrel-chested, muscular shooter will usually require more pitch than will a slim person. Women as a general rule will require more pitch than will men. The bustier the woman, the more she will benefit from an increased angle of pitch. Most men will find three to five degrees of pitch will suit them quite well. Women will usually be more comfortable with between five and eight degrees of pitch. A problem that seems to occur all too frequently is someone shortening a stock with no consideration to pitch. The scenario may go something like this: A well-intentioned husband is trying to interest his wife in wing-shooting. He knows enough about gun fit to realize that his wife, who is several inches shorter and many pounds lighter, will not be comfortable shooting one of his guns. She obviously needs a shorter length of pull. He makes the supreme sacrifice and cuts down the stock of one of his guns. His intentions are good, but his knowledge of gun fit is lacking. He sets the miter gauge on his table saw at ninety degrees and cuts off whatever amount he has deemed appropriate to make the gun more comfortable for his wife. She now finds it much easier to bring the gun to shoulder, and he feels like a real hero. The problem arises when he takes her out to shoot. After only a few shots she complains that the toe of the stock is digging into her chest, and she doesn't want to shoot anymore. The male chauvinism in him wells up, and he kicks himself for having cut the stock in the first place. If he had only been aware of pitch and cut the stock at an angle of six or seven degrees, his wife probably would not have been bothered by the recoil.

The shape of the buttstock can further affect how the recoil is distributed. Some stocks are designed with a slight concavity at the butt. This concavity gives the stock a graceful appearance, but it can make the gun uncomfortable for some to shoot. The problem is that the toe of the stock becomes more pointed as the degree of concavity increases, and this has a tendency to cause the toe to dig into the chest when the gun is fired. Women generally find that this stock design is best avoided. Women generally prefer a stock with a straight butt and a slightly rounded toe.

Pitch also affects how high a gun will shoot. Increasing pitch will make a gun tend to shoot lower; decreasing pitch will make it tend to shoot higher. This difference is most easily visu-

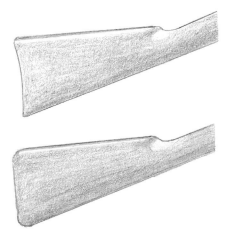

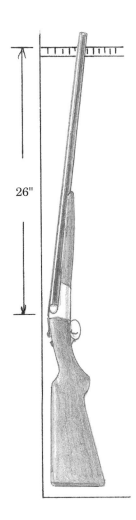

A slightly concave butt lends a graceful line to a stock, but can be uncomfortable for some shooters. A stock with a rounded toe is usually more comfortable, particularly for women shooters.

Measuring pitch in inches rather than degrees can be achieved by standing the gun on its butt and measuring the distance the barrels stand away from a vertical surface.

alized if we imagine the gun being anchored firmly on the shoulder and then increasing or decreasing the pitch. As we change pitch we are changing the angle of the barrels relative to the butt. If the pitch is increased and the butt held firmly on the shoulder, the barrels will be angled down. Obviously, as pitch is decreased in this situation the barrels will be pointed higher. Some trap guns are designed with very little pitch, or even with a slight negative pitch. The techniques used in trapshooting are specialized, and some shooters feel that this style of stock gives them an advantage. Field gunners will usually find that a stock with between three and seven degrees of pitch will suit their purposes better.

Pitch can be measured in degrees of angle with the aid of a protractor or a tool made specifically for measuring stocks. But lacking either of these tools, you can measure pitch by another technique. Stand the gun on its butt and push the receiver up against a plumbed vertical surface such as a door jamb or a wall. By measuring the distance between the barrel and the vertical surface one can determine pitch. It is critical that this measurement be taken at a standard distance from the point where the breach meets the vertical surface. Obviously, if we take this measurement at the muzzle of a gun with thirty-two-inch barrels we will get a larger measurement than we would if we were to measure a gun with an identical stock equipped with twenty-six-inch barrels. In order to equate this system to degrees of angle, we must measure the distance the barrels stand away from our vertical surface at a point twenty-six inches from where the receiver touches that vertical surface. Using this system, one-half inch equals one degree of pitch. For example, most field guns are produced with four degrees of pitch; if this gun were stood on its butt and pushed up against a door jamb the muzzles would be two inches away from the jamb, presuming twenty-six-inch barrels.

Aside from the measurements thus far discussed, several other aspects of a stock can affect how it suits a shooter. The butt plate or recoil pad can affect how easily the gun comes to shoulder. Hard plastic or metal butt plates are strong and will not catch on clothing as the gun is raised to shoulder. The same holds true for checkered wood butts. None of these offers any relief from recoil, however. If you are not particularly recoil-sensitive, and most of your hunting does not involve lots of shooting, a hard butt plate or checkered wood butt will be most serviceable. Most upland hunters just don't have the opportunity to fire a great number of shots on a typical outing. They are restrained by bag limits and their hunting situation; the ammunition they use is typically light, and recoil is not a major issue.

Anyone using heavy loads or doing a lot of shooting will find a recoil pad helpful. A typical day in the field may involve no more than a dozen shots, but what about the day you decide to sharpen your eye on clay targets? A well-designed recoil pad can make most any gun more pleasant to shoot. When choosing a recoil pad for a field gun you have to be mindful of your style of shooting and the impact the pad may have on your gun mount. A pad that functions well on a skeet or trap gun or on a rifle may be a hindrance on a field gun. Many of the recoil pads produced today are designed for competitive-style shooters. These shooters want a pad that will soften the blow and will stay put on the shoulder. Trap and skeet are most often shot with a preshouldered gun. Once the gun is positioned on the shoulder and cheek the skeet and trap enthusiast does not want it to slide about on the shoulder. Rifle shooters have a similar requirement; once their rifle is in position they do not want it to slide about. Ventilated rubber recoil pads with a pebble-like finish fill the needs of most competitive clay

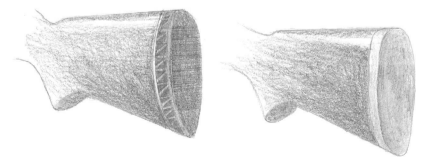

A smooth rubber- or leather-covered recoil pad is less likely to catch on clothing as the gun is mounted. The ventilated, pebble-finish rubber pads have a tendency to cling to clothing as the gun is shouldered.

A straight grip is preferred with double triggers and is perfectly suitable for a single trigger as well.

Pistol grips work well with a single trigger but can make double triggers more difficult to use.

target and rifle shooters. However, this style of recoil pad is not ideal for a field shooter because it tends to catch on clothing as the gun is brought to shoulder. Field gunners must mount their gun in one smooth motion. There is no time to preshoulder the gun and fidget until the correct position is attained. A recoil pad that clings to the shooter's jacket or vest can be a real nuisance. A field gun should have a smooth recoil pad that will slip over clothing easily. The solid rubber pads with a smooth surface are better suited to a field gun. Perhaps the best of all are the leather-covered recoil pads. They are smooth and will not cling to your clothing as you mount the gun to shoulder. The leather-covered recoil pads are more expensive to have installed than are the typical rubber pads, but the extra expense can be written off over many seasons of enjoyment in the field.

Another choice in stock design that should be considered is pistol grip versus straight grip. If the gun has a single trigger, I don't believe there is any significant difference in function.

Choose whatever style stock feels most comfortable to your hand. If the gun has double triggers, then I feel a straight grip is advisable. To best operate double triggers, the trigger hand should be free to move ever so slightly. A pistol grip makes double triggers more difficult to use because it restricts the mobility of the trigger hand. With the straight grip a shooter can more easily shuffle the trigger hand back to operate the rear trigger.

Some people theorize that the straight grip creates a more natural alignment between the hands. The hands seem to work together most naturally when they are held in the same plane, and the straight grip keeps the trigger hand closer to the line of the lead hand. I would not argue with the theory, but neither would I give it too much credence. Choose the grip shape that fits your hand best. This is just one of the many factors that determines whether the gun feels right to you, and that, in the final analysis, is what is critical: The gun must feel right.

Whenever I do a gun fit I tell shooters that they need to be an active participant in the process. The more experienced the shooter, the more crucial the input. I haven't seen one lately, but shoe salespeople used to have a item called a Brannock Device that you put your foot on that allowed them to determine your shoe size. But no matter what the device indicated your size might be, what was critical was to try the shoes on. Walk up and down the aisle of the store and be sure they felt right. Certainly we all have spent more time walking around in shoes than we have spent wingshooting, but don't sell yourself short. Particularly if you are a seasoned wingshooter, your sense of the gun's feel should be welcomed by the fitter. An experienced, knowledgeable gun fitter will work with the shooter to arrive at a set of stock dimensions that will be comfortable and efficient.

The Master Eye   5

Should you shoot with both eyes open, or should you close one eye as you bring the gun to shoulder? The answer to this question is determined by the similarity in eye dominance and hand dominance, or lack thereof. Everyone is aware of hand dominance and undoubtedly aware of which is his or her dominant hand. We are also born with a visual dominance. One eye will tend to prevail, particularly when we are pointing. Because of the distance between our eyes, we can't use them both as we point. The finger, shotgun barrel, or whatever we are pointing with will be pulled into alignment between the stronger of our eyes and the object we are looking at. We do not control which eye will dominate. Eye dominance, like hand dominance, is something we are born with. What is important in wingshooting is that your eye dominance and hand dominance be uniform. It does not matter one whit whether you are right dominant or left dominant. What is important is that your eye dominance matches your hand dominance.

Assuming that your eye dominance and hand dominance are uniform, that is, right-handed and right-eyed, or uniform left dominant, shooting with both eyes open will usually give you the best advantage. With both eyes open your peripheral vision and your depth perception will be enhanced. If your eye dominance and hand dominance are dissimilar, right-handed and left-eyed or vice versa, there may be a compelling reason to close one eye. The controlling consideration is whether your strong hand and your strong eye are on the same side. Most shooters will find that their eye dominance and hand dominance are uniformly right or left, but it is critical that you be aware if you are cross-dominant.

How can you determine which is your master eye? Simply point at an object with both eyes open. If you are right-handed, close your left eye after pointing. If your finger is still aligned

When pointing at an object the alignment is made with only one eye, the master eye. As long as we are not holding a gun the issue of cross dominance is of little importance.

with the object with the left eye closed, this indicates right-eye dominance. Your right eye pulled your finger into position without any conscious thought process. To give yourself a better appreciation of the phenomenon, try the test again. This time, after pointing out the object with both eyes open, close your right eye. If you are right-eye dominant, you will find that with only the left eye open your finger will be pointed several inches to the right of the object you originally focused on.

If you are left-handed use the same test, but after having made your initial point with both eyes open, close your right eye. Presumably you will find that with just the left eye open you are still on target. Most people will find that their eye dominance and hand dominance are uniformly right sided or left sided. What if you do not? What if you are right-handed and find that

The shooter on the left is right-handed and right-eyed and is pointing his gun in the direction he is looking. The shooter on the right is cross-dominant, right-handed and left-eyed. He will shoot across his line of vision and consistently shoot left.

after pointing at an object with both eyes open and then closing
the left eye, you are no longer lined up? First, try the test again.
Don't jump to any conclusions. You may find it easier to determine eye dominance by using a piece of paper with a hole in it.
Cut a hole about the size of a nickel in the middle of a sheet of
paper. Hold the paper out at arm's length and use the hole in the
paper like a peep sight. Pick out a small object roughly twenty
feet away and center the object in the hole in the paper, being
sure to keep both eyes open as you do this. Now close your left
eye. If the object remains centered in the hole, you are right-eye
dominant. If the object disappears from view, you are left-eye
dominant. If you do determine that your eye dominance and
hand dominance are not uniform, don't despair. You can still become a great wingshooter.

If you are cross-dominant, you should not shoot from the
shoulder of your strong hand and keep both eyes open. If you do,
you will be frustrated. Your natural pointing reflex will not align
your gun with your line of sight. The gun will align naturally
with the line of sight only when the shooting shoulder is on the
same side as the dominant eye. When the shooting shoulder and
dominant eye are on opposite sides, the gun will be canted across
the line of sight. Cross-dominant shooters have three options.
First, they can learn to shoot from the shoulder of the weak
hand. Second, they can close the dominant eye as the gun is
mounted to the shoulder of the dominant hand. Third, they can
resort to a cross-over stock. Let's consider each option.

If the cross-dominant shooter can manage it, learning to
shoot from the shoulder of the weak hand is probably the best solution. Shooting will be most natural when the gun is shouldered
to the side of the dominant eye. Particularly if the shooter is
young and relatively new to wingshooting, I would encourage him
or her to try switching shoulders. Some people make the conver-
sion quite easily. It's not uncommon to discover people who were

probably naturally left-handed but who have been forced into a right-handed mold. To my knowledge it is impossible to force a change in eye dominance. Your parents, teachers, coaches, or drill sergeants may have been able to cajole or beat you into a right-handed mold, but eye dominance is not affected. In such a case the person is not truly cross-dominant. Some people are left-handed in all activities except shooting. Many times these people served in the military and were "persuaded" to shoot right-handed because of the design of the guns they were using. They continue to shoot from the right shoulder when they pick up a shotgun because of this military experience. In many of these instances the switch to the opposite shoulder is relatively easy.

What if the shooter has a difficult time mounting the gun to shoulder on the weak side? Some people are truly cross-dominant. They are strongly right-handed and have an equally strong left eye, or vice versa. They may find that attempting to mount the gun on the weak side is so cumbersome and unwieldy that they are unwilling to pursue it. I usually suggest that such shooters try closing their dominant eye as they mount the gun to their strong-side shoulder. For example, right-handed shooters who have a dominant left eye would mount their gun to their right shoulder and close their left eye as they did so. By closing the naturally dominant left eye they are forced to use their right eye for alignment. Many times shooters will find that squinting the dominant eye is enough to force their other eye to take over the alignment. If they can train themselves to do this it is an expedient solution to the problem of cross-dominance. Such shooters can use both eyes until the last moment. They can take advantage of peripheral vision and depth perception to locate the bird and judge its range. Only after they have made the decision to shoot and the gun starts toward the shoulder do they close the eye. Very little is sacrificed with this technique. Many cross-dominant shooters find that closing the dominant eye just prior to mounting the gun to the strong-side shoulder is the most expedient way to deal with their problem.

But some people find it nearly impossible to close their dominant eye without closing both eyes. They cannot wink their strong eye. Such shooters might try wearing glasses with a piece of tape near the top of the lens on the side of the dominant eye. Obscuring the vision of the master eye in such a fashion could be tried by any cross-dominant shooter. I wouldn't be inclined to resort to this technique unless I had exhausted the aforementioned solutions first. The problem with taping over the lens of a shooter's glasses is deciding how much to obscure. If you totally block the vision of one eye you lose depth perception and compromise peripheral vision. Many people feel very uncomfortable if you put too much tape on their glasses. They feel as though they are about to step into a hole or over a bank. Obviously, if you don't

A small piece of tape on the top portion of the lens of shooting glasses can sometimes help a cross-dominant shooter.

block the master eye sufficiently it may continue to dominate and cause all the misalignment problems. There is a happy middle ground, and I have seen many cross-dominant shooters respond beautifully to a piece of tape on their glasses. It was small enough to have minimal effect on their depth perception and peripheral vision, yet large enough to force the weak eye to make the alignment. If you decide to try using tape, put it close to the top of the lens. This placement will usually eliminate the feeling of vertigo because you can still see as you look down. It will not have a marked effect on your vision until you try to look through the top of the lenses, as you do when in shooting position. Experiment with the size and shape of the piece of tape and its position on the lens. I carry a roll of Scotch tape with me whenever I'm working with students in our schools. Many cross-dominant shooters will find that a small piece of Scotch tape on the lens of the dominant eye will be enough to force the weak eye into making the alignment. The slight blurring created by the Scotch tape is hardly noticeable until the gun is raised to shooting position.

The last resort for the cross-dominant shooter is a crossover stock. This style of stock has a severe bend or cast. The stock is bent to the degree that the barrels are brought into alignment with the eye opposite from the shoulder to which the gun is mounted. I consider this stock a last resort because of the difficulty in fitting this style of stock. I have never seen a try gun that had sufficient range of adjustment to be used for fitting cross-over stocks, although such a try gun might exist. Most experienced gun fitters can arrive at a reasonably accurate set of stock dimensions if they have several guns of different dimensions available and can watch a shooter mount them to shoulder. This educated guesswork is never as satisfactory as using a try gun, but it at least provides some guidance for the fitting process. The problem with trying to acquire a cross-over stock is that no gun fitter I know has a try gun suitable to the purpose or a variety of cross-over stocks for a prospective buyer to try. It is just not feasible to keep a variety of cross-over stocks on hand for the rare occasion when one might be needed. To compound the problem, the gun fitter would need stocks that were bent both left and right to accommodate everyone. Accurately fitting a shooter to a cross-over stock is a daunting task at best. If you as a shooter determine that there is no other solution to your problem of cross-dominance, be sure that your gun fitter is confident and experienced with the cross-over design.

Fortunately, the shooter who requires a cross-over stock is exceedingly rare. The vast majority of cross-dominant shooters can find a much simpler solution to their problem. The simplest solution of all, as mentioned, is to train yourself to close one eye as you mount the gun. Best of all, most people need not concern themselves with cross-dominance because their eye dominance and hand dominance are uniform. They can keep both eyes open and give it their best shot.

A subject that I broach with some hesitancy, because of a lack of any real science to back me, is the difference in strength of visual dominance between men and women. It has been my observation over the years that women's visual dominance is slightly less persistent than men's. That is to say, women seem more prone than men to switch visual dominance from time to time. Certainly the dominant eye of both men and women can be distracted or can get "lazy" at times and allow the "off" eye to become the aligning force. It has been my observation that age seems to affect the strength of our visual dominance as well. I have noticed that older shooters seem somewhat more likely to switch dominance than are younger shooters. The problem for all of us, regardless of age or gender, is that if a switch in visual dominance happens, the shooter is completely unaware.

I have watched students in our shooting schools suddenly begin to miss targets for no apparent reason. The scenario usually is as follows. After a couple of hours of instruction students have made significant strides and are shooting well. They have progressed through the basic steps and have developed a sound gun mount complemented by good timing and visual concentration. Suddenly, with no apparent change in technique, they begin to miss. The misses are typically consistent; right-handed shooters will sometimes begin to shoot left and a little high, or they may begin to shoot quite low. Wherever their miss may be directed, it is always consistent, and they shoot with conviction. That is, the shooters neither hesitate nor chase their target. They bring their gun smoothly to shoulder and cheek and shoot upon completion of the mount, just as they have been coached to do. Yet, in spite of what appears to be good form they are consistently missing by a wide margin. These are typically shooters who are tiring and may be experiencing a shift in eye dominance. After observing the pattern I ask the students to shoot a couple of shots with a preshouldered gun so that I can eliminate the variables inherent in the gun-mount process. If the pattern of missing is still evident when the students shoot with a preshouldered gun, I then ask them to close the "off" eye. That is, I ask the shooters to close the left eye if they are shooting from the right shoulder, and vice versa for left-handers. Doing this will many times correct the problem.

The shift in eye dominance seems to be related to fatigue. Perhaps this fatigue explains the increased tendency that older and female shooters exhibit for switching eye dominance. I am not casting aspersions at older and female shooters; I certainly am a member of one of those groups. And, yes, the older I get, the more I find my eye dominance in question.

As mentioned, when I have observed shooters seemingly experience a switch in eye dominance they have typically been shooting for several hours. The good news, or perhaps bad news, depending on your point of view, is that the majority of field hunting situations don't provide the volume of shooting necessary to tire us out. But if you are in a situation that provides a lot of shooting, and out of the blue you start missing, among the many variables that you need to consider is whether your normal eye dominance may have changed. If you are engaged in a long clay target practice session, and you suspect a shift of eye dominance may be plaguing you, try closing your "off" eye on a few shots and see if anything changes. If you start breaking targets consistently with the "off" eye closed and with no other change in technique, you may have had a shift of eye dominance. The problem is that, as in most aspects of wingshooting, it is difficult for us to be self-diagnostic. Self-diagnosing a possible temporary shift in eye dominance is the toughest of all to call.

I believe that female shooters' propensity for shifting eye dominance may be related to the amount of experience the average female student brings to the lesson. I would guess that 50 percent of the women I have coached had little or no shotgunning experience. Perhaps only 10 percent of the male students I have worked with could be similarly classified. If a person is not accustomed to looking over the barrel of a gun, the presence of the barrel in the field of vision can be distracting. I believe that the vision of the eye on the side of the shooting shoulder is sufficiently obscured as to force the off eye of an inexperienced shooter to take over and become the aligning eye. The weaker eye will take over if the vision of the master eye is obscured. New shooters sometimes align with the weak eye because they have mounted the gun clumsily and inadvertently blocked the vision of the strong eye. This phenomenon is usually temporary. As their gun-mounting technique improves and the shooters become more accustomed to looking over the gun barrel, the problem usually resolves itself.

Lead   6

There is little debate among wingshooters about the necessity for lead, but there is much debate about how to best establish the correct amount of lead. If you shoot clay targets in a controlled situation where target presentation is repeated, you can practice the shot and consciously develop a sight picture, or barrel–bird relationship, that is appropriate for that presentation. You can, through trial and error, work out the necessary lead. The field gunner's problem is a lack of predictability, which prevents her from practicing particular shots. The conscious leads that may be developed in a clay target situation are difficult to apply in the field. The field gunner is better served by a more instinctive style that will accommodate the spontaneity of that world.

The Churchill, or instinctive, system is designed to build the lead into the gun mount and swing and establish the necessary lead without the shooter being aware of the exact amount of that lead. It relies on the eye's instinctive capabilities and a gun-mounting style that will incorporate lead into the swing. The gun-mounting style is designed to create sufficient momentum in the gun and the shooter to carry the muzzles through the target and automatically establish the correct lead. It does not require the shooter to calculate the lead consciously. The theory is that the speed of the target will determine the amount of momentum in the swing. A fast-moving target will require shooters to swing their body and gun rapidly and thereby develop sufficient momentum to carry their gun well beyond the target as the shooters fire. A slow-moving bird requires less speed and therefore less momentum. The gun will swing through the bird only a modest amount.

Establishing lead is a by-product of a good swing, just as surely as hitting a golf ball straight down the middle of the fairway is a by-product of a good swing. Everything from the stance on up contributes to the overall success. Lead cannot be discussed out of context; it is part of the whole. Unfortunately, most shooters consider lead to be a topic separate from gun mount, stance, hand placement, timing, or any of the other aspects of good wingshooting technique. Lead is not something you add on just before pulling the trigger. Just the opposite is true for the field gunner. Lead should be a natural outflow of a properly executed swing.

Shooters use several terms to describe the various systems for establishing lead. Many shooters use what they term a "sustained lead technique." They move the shotgun barrel a predetermined distance out in front of the target and try to maintain this carefully measured distance as they shoot. If the situation is a controlled one like skeet, where speed, angle, and range are known, this system can be an effective way to shoot. The system is not well suited to most field shooting, with the possible exception of some types of pass shooting. If shooters can see the target at sufficient distance to allow them time to judge range and speed, they might be able to calculate the lead necessary. Particularly if they have the opportunity to shoot from the same blind or in the same area for a number of years, they might log enough experience to give them a good feeling for leads necessary for particular shots. But in general the sustained lead technique is not an easy one to apply in the field. Walk-up, or upland, hunting does not lend itself to the sustained lead technique, and I don't recall ever hearing anyone champion it for any situation other than pass shooting.

Snap, or spot, shooting is a system that some people deem to be more appropriate to upland hunting. Rather than swing their gun along at a predetermined distance out in front of the target, snap shooters poke their gun to a spot well out in front of the target, stop, and attempt to pick it off as it passes in front of the muzzles. This impulse can be a very strong one for some shooters. Snap shooting appears to be a logical and relatively easy way to down a bird that is crossing or incoming. Shooters would seem to gain an advantage if they prepositioned their gun in the path of the oncoming bird. Perhaps the impulse is some ancient ambush mentality left over from our hunter-gatherer past. Snap shooting can be done, but it is more difficult than it would appear. If your gun is keeping pace with the target, as in the sustained lead technique, timing is less critical. But if the gun is stopped and the target is crossing, you have created a shooting situation that requires split-second timing—timing too demanding for most of us.

Let's consider a target that is crossing at a ninety-degree angle at thirty yards from the gun and traveling thirty miles an hour. Typically the muzzle velocity of a charge of shot is twelve hundred feet per second. If we disregard the deceleration of the shot over the thirty yards, the shot will take 0.075 second to reach the target. During the 0.075 second the target would travel 3.3 feet. This distance is the amount of lead we need. Providing you were able to ascertain speed, angle, and range and make the calculation for lead, you would still need near-perfect timing to make the snap shooting technique work. If you err by as little as one-tenth of a second, you will miss. A sustained lead practitioner, by contrast, has some margin for error in regard to timing because the muzzles are presumably traveling along about three and one-half feet in front of the target. For the field gunner, the obvious problem with both the sustained lead and the snap shooting systems is the necessity for calculating lead.

Swing-through is another technique for establishing lead. This technique is in some regards similar to that of the Churchill system. Swing-through shooters mount their gun to shoulder and initially point the gun slightly behind or at the tail of the bird. They then sweep the muzzles past the target and fire as the gun is pulling away in front. The swing-through technique has various forms. Some shooters fire as soon as they see daylight between the barrel and the bird. Others hold fire until the barrel is a predetermined distance out in front. The latter variation comes close to a sustained lead system. It requires shooters to be conscious of the amount of lead they are using.

Many shooters mount the gun to shoulder before making any lateral motion, or swing. This shooter has completed the gun mount too early.

In the basic form of swing-through, practitioners are not conscious of how much they are leading their target. They pull the muzzles through the target and fire as soon as they are in front. This technique is similar to that of the Churchill system in that it relies on gun momentum to establish the lead. The Churchill system is, in my opinion, a refinement of the swing-through system. We might more accurately call the swing-through technique a variation of the Churchill system, but however you look at it, the two techniques are similar.

Although similar, the two techniques have differing elements that, in my opinion, make the technique of the Churchill system preferable, particularly with respect to its applicability to the demands of the field shooter. The two techniques differ principally with regard to where the muzzles are aligned at the completion of the gun mount. The Churchill system requires the shooter to swing through the bird at the end of the gun mount and fire without hesitation. Most swing-through advocates in this country suggest completing the gun mount and then moving

The swing and the mount must be integrated. We must train ourselves to start the gun and body moving along with the target as we mount the gun to shoulder. The gun should not meet the cheek until the last instant when the shot is taken.

through the bird. The target is passed subsequent to the completion of the gun mount in the swing-through technique. The Churchill system asks the shooter to pass the target during the gun mount. I may seem to be splitting hairs, but the difference is a significant one. Swing-through shooters bring their gun fully to cheek and shoulder and intentionally point the muzzles behind the bird. Their next step is a swing that will carry the gun beyond the bird as they fire. This technique does not take best advantage of our natural pointing abilities. Shooters have used their natural pointing gesture to direct the gun to the wrong spot, behind the bird. Also, shooters must now make their swing with the barrels in the middle of their field of vision.

Wouldn't it be easier to start the swing as the gun is coming up to the shoulder? Start the lateral motion, or swing, at the beginning and build it into the gun mount, rather than add it at the end. When a bird flushes, or swings over the decoys, our first response should not be to snap the gun to cheek and shoulder, as is so frequently the case. We must train ourselves to start the gun moving along with the bird and keep the body square to the direction of fire. In this way the gun mount and swing are integrated. Shooters keep their eye riveted on the bird and push their lead hand (left hand for right-handed shooters) at the target as though they were pointing at it. Shooters have the impression that they are shooting directly at the target, but, in fact, the momentum of their swing carries them beyond the target as the gun is fired. With this style of gun mount you take best advantage of your instinctive pointing abilities and decrease the likelihood of being visually distracted by your gun. Your gun is not in the middle of your field of vision until the last instant, and this is the instant when you should take the shot.

If you can steel yourself and suppress the reflex to snap your gun fully to shoulder as a preliminary to any other motion, you will be well on the way to developing a swing that will carry your gun through the target. The key is learning to swing through rather than just to the target. You are striving to develop a system that will build lead naturally into the swing, a system that will naturally lead the bird and not require you to consciously calculate lead and add it at the end of the process.

I have heard the Churchill, or instinctive, system described as one that eliminates lead. This description is, of course, incorrect. The only way to decrease the necessity to lead our target is to increase the speed of the shot charge. The Churchill system can only make the lead seem more natural. In practice, we are

No matter what the angle, we must suppress the reflex to snap the gun to shoulder as a preliminary to any other motion. The gun must come to shoulder smoothly and meet the cheek only at the very last instant when the shot is taken.

not conscious of the amount we are leading the bird. We may actually be left with the impression that we shot directly at the bird because our visual attention remains focused there. We must be careful not to be misled. Field gunners must point their lead hand and gun muzzle through the target, not just to it.

Most inexperienced shooters have a tendency to tighten up and look down at the barrels at the instant of fire. Doing this will stop your swing and cause you to shoot behind your target in most cases. You must train yourself to keep your eye on the bird and flow through the target with a relaxed, smooth swing. Students of golf and tennis have a similar problem. At the critical instant when they are about to make contact with the ball, they have an inclination to tighten up and look up. "Relax, keep your eye on the object you are trying to hit, and follow through" is advice that could be given to students of any eye-hand activity.

As range increases, it is important to remind ourselves that we are not shooting directly at the target. Again, we may be left with that impression because of our visual concentration on the bird, but the momentum of our swing is, in fact, carrying us beyond the bird at the instant of fire. We must allow our gun to flow through and beyond the bird as we fire. The trick, if we may call it that, is to allow the momentum in our swing to carry the barrels out in front of the target but not to allow ourselves to become fixated on how far out in front we may be. This advice may sound strange, but it is at the heart of an accomplished field shooter's technique. As range increases, shooters become increasingly aware that their gun has passed the bird as they fire, but they cannot tell you exactly how much they have led each bird. If you try to engineer the shot too precisely, you will usually end up breaking your visual lock on the target and miss.

Something I remind myself of, particularly when faced with long crossing or overhead shots, is what is coming out of my shotgun. We have a tendency to conceptualize our shooting in two-dimensional form, as though we could accurately re-create it on a piece of paper. Particularly when we think about the pattern that our gun is delivering at any given range, we tend to fall into this two-dimensional mind-set. Countless students have asked me how wide their pattern of shot was at whatever distance we happen to be shooting. But in thirty-plus years, not one has asked me how long their column of shot might be at the range they were shooting. We tend to focus on the width of the pattern and disregard its depth. But what is coming out of our gun is not a two-dimensional spray of pellets. If we fire our gun at a patterning board we see the imprint left by the shot striking the surface. The column of shot that leaves this two-dimensional imprint had, in all likelihood, greater depth than diameter. The charge of shot delivered at typical shotgun range does not look like a dinner plate but is, in fact, a column of shot. The distance between the front and the rear of the shot column is generally greater than the pattern's breadth.

The length of the shot column relative to its breadth is affected by a number of variables, including shot size, degree of choke, gauge, and type of shot, to mention but a few. What is important from a wingshooter's point of view is that not all the shot arrives at the target at the same time. Remind yourself that if the first pellet at the head of the column strikes your bird dead center, much of the shot column will fall behind. This fact is particularly true of crossing or high birds overhead. Remind yourself to execute your swing with a push of the lead hand that will carry your gun through the target as the shot is taken. Your mind-set should be to have a swing that will flow through your bird such that the first few pellets at the head of the shot column will cross just in front of your target. What is important is that your swing be fluid and have a natural continuity.

If shooters become overly conscious of the gap between barrel and bird, they will many times stop their swing. Visually we must stay locked on the bird. Upland shooting seldom allows time for us to become overly conscious of anything. Pass shooting generally gives us more time to think about the shot and thereby a greater likelihood that we will confuse ourselves. The bird that can be seen from a long distance is often the most difficult target. We raise our gun prematurely and try to measure everything too precisely. In our attempt to align everything down to the last millimeter, we break visual concentration on the target, focus on the gap between barrel and bird, and end up stopping our swing. As we pull the trigger we may have the feeling that this one is as good as in the bag. In most cases we will shoot behind the bird.

Lead is present in most every situation, whether you are shooting bobwhite quail or ruffed grouse in thick cover or pass shooting geese or dove. At moderate range lead comes so naturally that we may think it has vanished entirely; it hasn't. If your swing is made properly, and if you keep your eye on the bird, the lead is built in. What we must be mindful of is not to take it out. All too frequently I have peered over the shoulders of students and watched as they executed the shot beautifully until the last second. Their technique was good, and the lead was perfect, but at the last instant they broke confidence and tensed up. At the end of a well-executed swing they lacked the confidence to pull the trigger. Instead, they rode their bird, trying to see exactly what the lead was. They ended up focused on the barrel as they pulled the trigger; the swing stopped, and they shot behind the bird.

Confidence is an important ingredient in all eye-hand activities, and wingshooting is no exception. Attitude is particularly important in pass shooting situations when there is time to think. Have you ever noticed that the unexpected shot is the one you often make? A bird flushes when you least expect it, and without any thought your gun comes to shoulder, and the shot is fired. Your hunting companion is duly impressed by your style, and you modestly say, "Guess I got lucky on that one." It wasn't luck; it was the fact that the bird caught you by surprise and totally captured your attention. Your eye and hand worked together unimpeded by the wheels between your ears.

Pass shooting waterfowl, hunting dove, and making driven bird shoots are situations in which the bird is often seen well before it is in shotgun range. Staying relaxed and confident as you watch the bird approach is critical to success. If you can channel your energies visually, you will improve your score. Train yourself to see the bird clearly enough to be able to identify detail. Don't see the whole bird—look for a specific part of the bird. Force yourself to look at the bird's eye or beak. It is of little consequence what detail on the bird you focus on, but I would suggest something on the eating end. If you look at a part rather than the whole, you will be less likely to break your visual lock on the target. Like the golfer staring at just one dimple on the ball, the wingshooter can gain an edge in concentration by focusing on a detail. If we can maintain this high degree of visual concentration, it seems to occupy the mind and prevents us from overthinking the shot.

Be able to accept a miss. No one in the history of wingshooting has an unblemished record. Mulling over a miss will only destroy your confidence and thereby, many times, your timing. Often students have turned to me in disgust and said, "What happened? I know I was on that one." They many times have been correct, but not in the manner they meant. Yes, they may have thought they had been dead-on, but they had stopped their swing. They had taken a little extra time at the end of the process to really aim their shot. Their gun stopped because they were looking at the bead rather than at the bird. They missed a couple of targets and were trying to be too precise. They were fretting over a miss and allowing themselves to revert to an aiming technique. Do not allow a miss or two or three to shake your confidence in the system. Do not allow a miss to make you question your ability to point your gun accurately. You must shoot with confidence. The shooter who shoots confidently with one free-flowing motion will always be most successful.

Don't be overly self-critical while in the field, particularly with regard to where you may have missed. If you try to figure out where you missed each bird, you will be in for a long day of figuring. Students who want to know where they missed every shot are missing the point. They are still thinking in terms of aiming. The way to hit the next bird is not by compensating for a mistake you made on the last bird. Even if you are consistently shooting high or low or wherever it may be, the way to correct your problem is not by consciously aiming to the opposite side. The way to correct your problem is by finding the flaw in technique or in the fit of your gun. If you are consistently shooting high, perhaps you have too much weight on your back foot, or perhaps your lead hand is too far forward. You may not be checking your gun firmly enough, or the gun may not have sufficient drop to suit you. Find out why, not where; there is an enormous difference.

We all are going to miss an occasional target; we may even miss several. The way to get back on track is not to guess where we missed and build a conscious aiming correction into subsequent shots. The way to get back on track is to review in your mind what a good shot looks like. Remind yourself of the basics of good wingshooting technique. I tell all our students they should have a mental image of a well-executed gun mount–swing sequence. I personally have a cartoon strip–like image I use to try to get myself back on track. The first frame is an illustration of a shooter in a good ready position. This frame is to remind myself to be sure I am standing up straight and not crouching. All too frequently shooters will begin to hunch over, rolling their shoulders in and dropping their head as they tense up after several misses. The second frame is the same image as the first, with the addition of the bird we are shooting at and a lightning bolt going from the shooter's eye to the bird. This frame is intended to remind me to be sure I am seeing my target clearly before I attempt to shoot it. Frequently shooters who have missed a couple of targets will get jumpy. They will mount their gun fully to shoulder before their eye has had an opportunity to lock on the bird. The third frame shows the shooter with a properly mounted gun: stock in contact with the underside of the cheekbone, lead hand well extended, and a slight weight shift in the direction that the bird is traveling. Hopefully, this frame will remind me to move smoothly, to resist the tendency to overreact to the target as a consequence of anxiety spawned by a miss. The last frame is a close-up of the trigger finger pulling the trigger. This frame is a reminder to shoot with confidence; keep your eye on the bird's beak and shoot when you feel the pressure of the stock on the underside of your cheekbone. Resist the inclination to ride the bird at the end of the sequence and end up focusing on the barrel. Don't let a miss get into your head and chase you around all day. Forget the miss; review the basics of good style in your mind; and most importantly keep your eye on the *bird*.

Safety and Shooting Etiquette

Teaching people how to hit what they are shooting at is what this book is all about, but there is a much more important issue inherent to every shooting situation: how to prevent shooting something you didn't intend to hit. Before people attempt to learn how to shoot they must have thorough knowledge of gun safety. Firearms can be dangerous, just as automobiles can be dangerous. If firearms are used properly with good judgment and common sense prevailing, there is no reason to fear them. If they are put into the wrong hands and used carelessly, there is potential for harm. All in all, I feel a lot safer when I am in the field hunting than when I am on a crowded highway.

Hunter safety courses are mandatory in most states before a hunting license will be issued; as my grandfather was so fond of saying, "So mote it be," and a hearty amen. People should not pick up a firearm until they have a thorough understanding of its safe operation. Hands-on instruction is required. I would not want any new shooters to read a few pages in this book, or in any other, and feel they were ready to load and fire.

The basic rules of gun safety are simple. Never point a gun at anything you don't intend to shoot, and treat every gun as though it were loaded until you can positively verify that it is not. Gun safety is common sense and courtesy. The action of your gun should be kept open and empty except when actively hunting or when on the firing line at the practice range. If there is a question in your mind about any situation, err on the side of caution. Don't be in too big a hurry to load your gun whether afield or at the practice range. The shooter who is stuffing shells into his gun before the truck door is closed will never get another shooting invitation from me. Never hurry when around firearms; take your time; be in control at all times.

In my experience, most people are very aware of the basic rules of gun safety. Rare indeed is the shooter who truly is not aware. *Careless* is the operative word. Of the hundreds of shooters I have dealt with, only a handful were truly careless, but it takes only one. Never be reticent about reminding shooters if they become careless. Carelessness is not a situation that calls for diplomacy; be polite, but be direct.

A number of years ago I witnessed a shooter being justifiably rebuked for taking dangerously low shots. It was on a driven shoot in Europe, and the shooter was shooting too close to the line of beaters. The gamekeeper of the estate on which we were shooting pointed this out to the shooter, who was understandably very embarrassed. I don't believe the fellow in question was so much reckless as he was excitable. This was a new experience for him, and he wanted to put in a good performance. The lesson is this: Never be embarrassed to hold your fire. No bird in the world is worth taking a risky shot for. If for any reason you don't feel totally comfortable and in control, don't shoot. This advice is particularly important in new situations. Ease into it. I tell students in our wingshooting schools that I will always respect their decision not to fire. Never feel pressured to shoot.

Another aspect of gun safety is the proper care and maintenance of your gun to ensure that it does not malfunction and injure you or anyone else. The most common accident in this vein for the shotgunner is caused by an obstruction in the barrel. It takes only a little bit of mud or snow to plug a shotgun barrel with disastrous consequences. I make it a habit to check the barrel before loading. I prefer breaking-style guns over magazine-style guns for several reasons, and among the reasons is the ease of detecting any foreign object in the barrels when loading.

Not only must we be careful to prevent the muzzle from becoming obstructed, but also we must be careful of what goes in from the breech end. A roll of LifeSavers, a roll of Tums, or a tube of Chapstick all feel rather like a shotgun shell if they are fished out of a pocket hurriedly. If the shooting is fast, as it can be in the dove field or on a driven shoot, the gun may be loaded more by feel than by sight. If the roll of whatever falls through the chamber and lodges in the barrel, shooters may not realize what has happened. When they raise their gun, and it fails to fire they may think they dropped their shell on the previous loading attempt. When they open their gun it appears to be empty because the obstruction is not visible. It has passed through the chamber and is lodged partway down the barrel. If they do not take time to check the bore before loading a live shell, the stage has been set for disaster. This scenario may sound far-fetched, but it has happened. Don't let it happen to you. If you experience a misfire, always point the gun in a safe direction and wait fifteen or twenty seconds before opening the action. After ensuring that the gun is unloaded, inspect the bore before loading another shell.

Never mix ammunition of any type in your pocket. The Tums scenario could just as likely, or perhaps even more likely, have involved a smaller-gauge shell. A twenty-gauge shotgun shell will fall through the chamber of a twelve-gauge gun and lodge in the barrel. A twelve-gauge shell may then be loaded, and the gun will fire. I don't believe it is necessary to go into gory detail about the consequences. Suffice it to say that this scenario could result in severe injury or death. A twenty-eight-gauge shell will have the same effect if mistakenly loaded into either a twenty- or a sixteen-gauge gun. Carry only the ammunition appropriate for the gun you are using.

Never fire a shotgun loaded with ammunition longer than the chamber was designed for. Shotguns are made with different chamber lengths. Most shotgun ammunition manufactured today is designed for use in guns with chambers two and three-quarters inches or longer. Most modern shotguns have chambers of either two and three-quarters or three inches, but over the years many guns were produced with shorter chambers. Chambers as short as two inches have been used in some European guns, and chambers of two and one-half and two and nine-sixteenths inches are not rare. You can't determine whether a shell is appropriate for the chamber by measuring an unfired shell and relating that to the chamber length of your gun. What is important is the length of the shell after it has been fired, when the crimp has opened. Just because a shell will readily fit into your gun does not ensure that your gun is designed to use that shell. A three-inch shell can be loaded into a gun with a chamber of two and three-quarters inches, but it should never be fired.

Know what the chamber length of your gun is. If the chamber length is not marked clearly on the barrel or action, take your gun to a knowledgeable gunsmith or gun dealer and let that person determine the chamber length. If your gun has a chamber of two and three-quarters inches, you may shoot that length or any shorter shell, but never fire three-inch shells in the gun. Use three-inch loads only if your gun has a chamber of three inches or longer. Your gun may not explode or show immediate signs of damage if you use ammunition only slightly longer than the chamber—for example, if you fire ammo of two and three-quarters inches in a gun with a chamber of two and one-half or two and nine-sixteenths inches. But the gun will be stressed beyond the limits it was designed to tolerate. The pressure in the chamber will be greater than it was designed to work under. You will damage the gun and risk injury to yourself if you persist in using ammunition longer than the gun was made for.

If you purchase a used gun, be sure it is in sound working order before firing it. Be sure the gun was proof-tested for the ammunition you intend to use. If purchasing an older double, be aware of the difference between modern fluid steel and Damascus steel in barrels. Ammunition produced today uses smokeless powder and should not be fired in a gun with Damascus steel barrels. If all this sounds confusing, have a competent gunsmith inspect any used gun you are considering before handing over the money. Even more important, don't fire the gun until it has been inspected by a knowledgeable person.

I strongly suggest another precaution. Do not fire any gun unless you are wearing some type of protective eyeglasses. If an accident should occur, your eyes are most vulnerable. The best pair of shooting glasses you can buy is mighty cheap insurance. Along the same line, I strongly suggest the use of some type of hearing protection. Hearing protection is not accident insurance, but rather a means of protecting ourselves from the damage that is done to our hearing every time we are subjected to a very loud noise. You will eventually lose your sense of hearing if you don't shield your ears in some manner. Either ear plugs or ear muff–style protectors should be used. Many types of hearing protection are on the market, but just be sure that, whatever type you select, you are comfortable with it when shooting. No matter how many bells and whistles your hearing protection may have, if it is not comfortable to shoot in, you probably will not wear it. Hearing protection is particularly important at practice sessions where you are likely to do more shooting than in the field, and you will probably be close to other shooters.

I have to admit that I do not use hearing protection when upland hunting. Our New England grouse and woodcock shooting seldom heats up the barrels with action. Even if more shooting were involved, I doubt I would use any type of hearing protection. The reason is that hearing is important to the experience, particularly when hunting in heavy cover. You need to be able to hear the bell or beeper on your dog's collar. You often hear a bird flushing before you see it, if you see it at all. Hearing is essential to the experience, so we unfortunately have little choice but to sacrifice a bit of the sense we so depend on every time we go afield. If hearing is not essential to the game, as in practice sessions, driven bird shoots, or dove hunts where you are also more likely to be exposed to a greater volume of shooting, by all means protect your hearing.

I want to reemphasize the necessity of learning safe gun-handling practices first-hand from a qualified instructor. Do not go to the practice range or to the game field until you have had the benefit of personal instruction from a qualified person.

Tools 8

Most people have seen American folk-art prints depicting a barefoot boy with cane pole, worm can, and full stringer of fish, in counterpoint to a well-dressed and well-equipped angler fruitlessly plying the same stream. A quaint bit of Americana, but have you ever known a bent-pin fisherman who, by virtue of his pin, was more successful than the well-equipped angler? Stories of barefoot kids outfishing and outhunting their well-equipped adult counterparts seem to be part of the lore of American field sports. Understandably, no one wants to play the role of the overequipped, hapless dandy. We all would prefer to think of ourselves as the barefoot kid who, by virtue of native skill, can outshoot, outfish, and outanything the overequipped slicker attempts.

Why is this barefoot boy syndrome so common among shooters? I have known people who seem to pride themselves on the shabbiness of their hunting clothes. Most of these people would not consider mowing their lawn, much less going to the golf course, while similarly dressed. Some shooters exhibit a similar attitude toward their gun. They seem to feel that an inexpensive, beat-up old gun is a badge of honor. If you are of the barefoot boy school, ask yourself what the kid who outshot the well-equipped shooters with his old, ill-fitting gun could have done if he had had good equipment.

Good equipment is nothing to be embarrassed about. A fine gun will not instantly transform a mediocre shooter into an expert, but a fine gun will help everyone shoot better. An ill-fit, ill-balanced gun will handicap everyone. I can find no virtue in choosing to dress shabbily and shoot an old clunker. Most of us can't afford a best-grade London sidelock, but buy the best you can afford. You don't have to spend a fortune to ensure a good-quality gun. The most important thing is not the price tag, but rather the fit. If you can afford a custom-fit gun, great; if you can't, shop until you find a production gun that fits well or can be altered to fit.

The relative merits of various types of shotguns have been the topic of much discussion. Autoloaders, pumps, over-unders, side-by-sides, and any other configuration of shotgun you can name has its loyal supporters. I am not inclined to add my two cents to the melee. If a person has confidence in a gun or in a particular type of action, that confidence is usually worth more than all the theoretical arguments. No one gun will suit every shooter's needs in every situation.

Although I don't intend to discuss the relative merits of the various shotgun actions, I will make one comparative observation. I am more at ease when those around me are using break-action guns. I am not suggesting that magazine-style guns are inherently more dangerous than breaking-action guns, but I am more guarded when our students are shooting autoloaders or pump-action guns. The reason is simple: The top lever on a breaking gun is easy to operate, and once the gun is open I can relax a bit. When the action is open, it is obvious if the gun is loaded or not. Although it is easy to open the action of an auto loader or a pump, there is still the question of whether there are shells in the magazine. It takes close scrutiny to determine if shells remain there. It also takes slightly more time and effort to remove the shells from the magazine of a pump or autoloader than to pluck them from the chambers of a side-by-side or over-under. It is easier to open and unload a breaking gun than a magazine gun, and for that reason more shooters seem inclined to do so. There can be no argument that the shooter, not the gun, determines how safe any situation will be. A responsible, thoughtful shooter will be safe no matter what style of gun they are using. A careless shooter can't be made careful by the use of a particular type of gun.

Rather than debate the relative merits of various shotgun types, I would like to offer an opinion on an issue that is pertinent to every shotgun action and yet has not received the attention it deserves. Most shooters consider barrel length to be related to the type of shooting they engage in. I contend that the length of the barrels used by shooters should be more related to the shooters' size and physique than to the shooting situation.

Conventional wisdom has been to use shorter barrels for upland hunting and longer barrels for water fowling. The notion that long barrels shoot farther or "harder" has been dispelled for the most part, as well it should be. Most people realize that with modern ammunition there is no ballistic necessity for barrels in excess of about two feet. Yet, most hunters will persist in using longer barrels when hunting water fowl than they use when hunting upland game. Why this custom persists is variously explained by the necessity for shorter barrels in the heavy cover to facilitate a quick swing or the advantage of a longer sighting plane when pass shooting ducks or geese. I'm not convinced of the efficacy of most of these explanations. If one accepts

Churchill's instinctive point technique and the necessity for total visual concentration on the target, the sighting plane explanation loses weight. The theory that a short barrel is always preferable in upland hunting does not agree with my experience.

The size and physique of the shooter should be the principal determinant of barrel length. The effect that barrel length has on balance and overall weight is more important than how far apart the trees are or any sighting radius arguments. Every knowledgeable shooter agrees that good balance is important in a shotgun. What constitutes good balance is a question for debate. Every shooter has his or her preference, but most people agree that the weight should be more or less evenly distributed between the hands. That is, the balance point of the gun should be approximately halfway between the points where the hands grip the gun. Some people prefer a gun that is a little barrel heavy, others prefer a gun that has less barrel weight, but the differences are subtle.

Once you decide what feels good to you, why change? Why change the weight and balance of your gun to conform to some outdated theory about longer barrels for the duck marsh? Hunters who switch from a twenty-six-inch barrel to a thirty-inch barrel have obviously changed the balance of their gun. Unless something is done to the stock to counteract the additional barrel weight, the balance point has been moved forward. If these same hunters are fortunate enough to own two guns, one for upland hunting and the other for waterfowl shooting, they may also have opted for a slightly shorter stock on their waterfowl gun. The heavy clothes often worn during the duck season add to the length of pull. If a gun is to be used while wearing heavy clothes it makes sense to decrease the length of pull a bit. If we decrease the length of pull and increase the barrel length, we shift the balance point forward and may end up with a gun that is very barrel heavy.

If our hypothetical two-gun hunters use a shorter barrel and longer stock on their upland gun than on their waterfowl gun, the feel of the two may become very different. If they use a short-barreled breaking gun with a long stock in the uplands and a long-barreled pump action or autoloader with a short stock in the duck blind, they are dealing with guns that have dramatically different balance and pointing characteristics. Be mindful of the impact that barrel length has on the handling and balance of your gun. The barrel length should be related to the length and weight of the stock. If you are small and require a short stock, be wary of excessively long barrels. Conversely, if you are taller than average and require a long stock, be careful not to use a barrel that is too short. The extremes are all we need to avoid. Do not move the balance point of the gun too far from a point halfway between your hands. Unfortunately, I have seen numerous shotguns that were poorly balanced; the two most common examples are autoloaders with shortened stocks and long barrels and breaking guns with longer-than-average stocks and short barrels.

The poorly balanced autoloader is usually created with the best intentions. A husband or father shortens the stock of an auto loader with a thirty-inch barrel to make the gun easier for a wife or child to shoot. Dad is an avid duck hunter and wants his wife or child to share his enjoyment. He knows enough about gun fit to realize the necessity of shortening the stock for his wife or child, but he is a firm believer in thirty-inch barrels. The gun that he's created is extremely barrel heavy. The young or female shooter trying to use this extremely unbalanced beast typically does not have the arm strength that dear old Dad has, and the combination is frustrating. If your length of pull is thirteen inches, you will probably not find thirty-inch or thirty-two-inch barrels comfortable, particularly on pumps or autoloaders. Conversely, if you use a fifteen-inch length of pull, be wary of twenty-five-inch barrels, particularly on breaking guns. I can remember shooting students who, in their attempt to create their "ulti-mate" upland gun, found frustration. Typically, taller and stronger-than-average shooters decide that their ultimate quail gun would be a five-and-one-half-pound over-under or side-by-side with twenty-five-inch barrels. They acquire such a gun and soon find that the standard fourteen-inch stock is much too short for them. They add a one-inch rubber recoil pad to lengthen the stock. This creates a better length of pull but moves the balance too far back. The gun is so muzzle light that the shooters have great difficulty moving smoothly. They typically start and stop the gun very quickly. The barrels feel too light. Longer barrels are not always better for the duck blind any more than shorter barrels are always better for upland hunting. Keep things in bal-ance as best you can. The length of barrel you use should be re-lated to the length of the stock.

Discussions centering around best choking and shot size for various situations have been numerous. The topic is important but, like the question of which action is best, not within the bounds of this book. I would refer readers to *Shotgunning: The Art and the Science* by Bob Brister. Certainly many knowledge-able authors have dealt with the subject, but I find Brister's in-sights most interesting. My experience as an instructor has led me to believe that most shooters tend to use too much choke rather than too little. This tendency is directly related to most folks' tendency to overestimate range. I occasionally ask stu-dents to estimate the distance they are shooting, and they are generally on the long side. This tendency is particularly true when the targets are overhead. One student told me that it would be nearly impossible to break a clay target at the range we were shooting with anything less than full choke. He was con-vinced that his improved cylinder choking was not adequate. Fortunately, another member of his group who was shooting an improved cylinder choke broke about 70 percent of the targets.

The student who was convinced he needed a full choke was fortunate to be in a controlled situation where the effectiveness of the open choke could be graphically demonstrated. Had he been in a dove field or duck blind he no doubt would have clung to his theory and probably gone out and bought a new gun or new barrel with full choke. His next outing would have been even more frustrating than the last. His margin for error would be significantly less with the full choke, and his likelihood of hitting anything would be decreased. Such shooters many times will try using larger shot on the theory that whatever they had previously been using was not capable of killing at this range. Don't allow yourself to fall into this trap. More choke and larger shot are seldom the solution for a wingshooter's ills.

Before you decide you need more choke, larger shot, or a new gun, determine if you are pointing your present gun in the right direction. Determining this is easier said than done, but all too frequently we blame the tools when the technique is at fault. There is no virtue in electing to use an ill-fit, clumsy gun, but even the best of guns must be pointed in the right direction. Good technique and good tools complement one another. We need them both to reach our full potential. The game we hunt deserves nothing less from each one of us.

Index

About the Author

Bruce Bowlen is director of the Orvis Shooting Schools. He lives in Dorset, Vermont.